LET ALL CREATION REJOICE:

REFLECTIONS FOR ADVENT, THE NATIVITY, AND EPIPHANY

BY
FR. STAVROS N. AKROTIRIANAKIS

Let All Creation Rejoice:
Reflections for Advent, the Nativity and Epiphany
by Fr. Stavros N. Akrotirianakis

Printed in the United States of America.

ISBN 9781498484077

www.xulonpress.com

Dedicated to my wife, Lisa
And to our son, Nicholas

Table of Contents

The Format of This Book

Most Christian churches have a period of time called "*Advent*." Advent is conventionally observed as a four-Sunday period before the feast of Christmas. In the Orthodox Christian Church, Advent is observed for forty days beginning on November 15. In the Orthodox Church the Feast of Christmas is called by various names including "*The Nativity*" and "*The Incarnation*." The term "*Christmas*" is seldom heard in Orthodox Christian circles. The Feast of the Nativity is celebrated for twelve days culminating in the Feast of Epiphany, or Theophany, as it is sometimes called.

This book has been written to be read on a daily basis from November 15 (the beginning of the Orthodox Advent season), through January 7 (the Feast of St. John the Baptist which falls one day after the Feast of Epiphany, which is held January 6).

The reflections of Advent focus on a verse or two from the scriptures on the Nativity, taken from Matthew 1 and 2, and from Luke 2. The reflections that follow the Feast of the Nativity focus on other scriptures related to the early life of Christ, culminating in His Baptism and the endorsement of St. John the Baptist.

Each reflection concludes with a hymn or prayer from Orthodox Christian services held for the Feasts of the Nativity and Theophany.

Acknowledgements

*I*n February, 2015, a parishioner approached me with an idea about creating a *prayer team*—a group of parishioners who would commit to praying for the church and for me during the upcoming Lenten period on a daily basis. I have always enjoyed writing and decided that for the period of Lent in 2015, I would write a daily reflection and send it to whoever joined the prayer team. I had hoped that thirty people would join and the intention was to do this for forty days. Over 150 people joined the Prayer Team and as Lent came to an end, they asked me if I would continue the daily reflections, and so I did.

When the season of Advent approached, I decided to dedicate the daily writings to the scriptures of Christmas and Epiphany. Encouraged by many to put these reflections in book form, I approached Xulon Press with this project.

I wish to thank those who have helped and encouraged me in this project:

His Eminence Metropolitan Alexios of Atlanta, the Greek Orthodox Bishop of the Metropolis of Atlanta, for his prayers and blessings;

To the many parishioners of St. John the Baptist Greek Orthodox Church in Tampa, FL, for their support of the prayer team and encouragement to move forward with this project;

To all the members of the Prayer Team, for reading my reflections, for your prayers, and for your encouragement;

To the Orthodox Christian Network (OCN) for posting my writings;

To an anonymous donor who provided the funds to make this project a reality;

To Father Anthony Salzman at www.imageandlikeness.com for his permission to use one of his icons as the front cover of the book;

To Father Seraphim Dedes for his permission to use his translations of the liturgical services;

To Dr. Anton Vrame at Holy Cross Greek Orthodox School of Theology for permission to use their translation of the liturgical services.

To my Mom for her encouragement and help, and for encouraging me from a young age to develop my writing skills;

To my son, Nicholas, who already enjoys writing, for his unconditional love, and for the endless stories he tells;

To my wife, Lisa, for her support of my ministry, for the many sacrifices she makes for our family, and her encouragement to write.

And most especially to the Lord, for the great blessing to serve as a Greek Orthodox priest, for giving me a talent to write, and a desire to share that gift through this project. I am thankful for the continued inspiration that He provides and this blessing He has given me to share my thoughts on the miracle of the Incarnation.

I can do all things through Christ who strengthens me.
—Philippians 4:13 (NKJV)

Introduction

Our Journey is about to Begin

Now faith is the assurance of things hoped for,
the conviction of things not seen.
—Hebrews 11:1

We are about to take a journey. Whether one is a devout Christian or doesn't know Christ at all, we are all about to take a journey that will see Christmas decorations go up, lines at the malls get long, and stress levels go up. Such is the modern celebration of Christmas.

But there is another journey, a journey of faith that some choose to take and others choose to ignore. The journey of faith is a daily choice to follow Christ. Each year on November 15, as we begin the Orthodox Christian season of Advent that journey takes on a new focus. For forty days, we prepare to celebrate the Nativity of Christ. We fast. We pray. We worship. When the Feast of the Nativity comes, there is something to celebrate. Most important, however, is that when the Feast of the Nativity has passed, there is something more than gifts to return, decorations to take down, and credit cards to pay off. There is joy—and joy is what overcomes sadness. There is hope—and hope is what overcomes sorrow.

So, I invite you to share a meaningful journey to Bethlehem this year. Over the next fifty-four days we will examine scriptures and services. We will study the characters in the Christmas story in a way that perhaps you haven't thought of them before. In preparing to do this project, in studying and praying over the scriptures, in trying to identify over fifty distinct topics from only a few chapters of scripture, I saw things in scripture that I never before slowed down to appreciate. The hustle and bustle of the season has even permeated how I've read these most important passages.

People greet the feast of Christmas in different ways—some are happy to see it come, and others dread its coming. And when Christmas is over, some are sad to see it go, while others are relieved. I feel blessed that, as an Orthodox priest, I celebrate Christmas all year round. Each time I celebrate the Liturgy and prepare the Gifts that will become the Body and Blood of Christ, I gaze upon an icon of the Nativity at the table of preparation (Prothesis) in the Holy Altar of the church. The first prayer of the service of the Preparation of the Gifts (the Proskomide) at every Eucharistic service (and we celebrate the Eucharist in a service called the Divine Liturgy over one hundred times a year) is a hymn of Christmas:

> O Bethlehem, prepare, Eden is opened unto all. And be ready, Ephrata, for the Tree of life has in the grotto blossomed forth from the Virgin. Indeed her womb is shown to be spiritually a Paradise, in which is found the God-planted Tree. And if we eat from it we shall live, and shall not die, as did Adam of old. Christ is born, so that He might raise up the formerly fallen image. (Trans. Fr. Seraphim Dedes.)

As I cover the Bread on the Paten with a metal covering *"asterisk,"* which looks like a four-point star, I offer a prayer based on the Gospel of Matthew 2:11: *"And the star came and stood over where the child was with Mary His mother."* (The prayer is found in *The Order of the Divine and Holy Liturgy* by Holy Cross Seminary Press)." The service concludes with the dismissal from the Nativity services, "May Christ our True God who was born in a cave and lay in a manger for our salvation . . ." So, it's always Christmas in the church. The lessons of the Nativity are things we should meditate on all the days of our lives.

The format of these daily writings will include some scripture, a short reflection, and a prayer. The prayers will be taken from services associated with the feasts of the Nativity and Epiphany. As we pass this Holy time of preparation, I humbly ask for your prayers. I humbly offer mine as well.

> O Bethlehem, welcome the Mother-city of God. For she is coming to give birth to the never-setting Light. Angels in heaven, marvel; people on earth, give glory. Magi from Persia, bring your triply precious gift. Shepherds in the field, sing the Thrice-Holy Hymn. Let everything that breathes praise the Lord who does all things. (From the Matins on the Feast of St. Andrew, November 30. Trans. Fr. Seraphim Dedes.)

Thank you for your interest in taking this journey together.

Prologue

In the Beginning

*In the beginning, **God created** the heavens and the earth. The earth was
without form and void, and darkness was upon the face of the deep; and
the **Spirit of God** was moving over the face of the waters. **And God said**
"Let there be light"; and there was light.*
—Genesis 1:1–3

Unlike our American culture, which celebrates from now until
Christmas, with celebrations ending promptly on December
26, the Orthodox Church celebrates the Nativity throughout the year.
Our joyful part of the celebration in this season is supposed to be from
December 25 through January 7. November 15 through December 24 is
a period of fasting and reflective preparation. The focus is neither shopping nor decorating, but meditating on the awesome miracle of the Son
of God taking on flesh and becoming one of us. This is why we call the
holiday either the Nativity (to commemorate an historical event) or the
Incarnation (to recognize the spiritual significance of the Nativity). Each
day of the forty days, we examine the scriptures of the Nativity. My hope
is that we'll take this journey together in a prayerful and purposeful way.

Today's "prologue" is a summary of what led up to the feast of the Nativity. Why did God send His Son to be among us? To answer this question, we go back to "the beginning."

In order to believe in God, one has to first believe that God created us—someone greater than us created us. Whether one interprets Genesis 1 as seven literal days or not (most Orthodox theologians affirm that the seven-day creation is an allegory), or whether one believes that God created everything, or that He created the first thing and a chain-reaction of evolutionary outgrowth was the result, the most important verses of Genesis 1 are the first three: In the beginning, God created the heavens and the earth. In the beginning, there was God, there was nothing else but God. And God created everything from nothing. God, however, is not created, but existed from the beginning.

In order to believe in Christ, one has to believe that He too, existed from the beginning. Genesis 1:1–3 reveals all three persons of the Holy Trinity, present and working together for the creation of the world. In the beginning God (the Father) created the heavens and the earth. The Spirit (Holy Spirit) of God was moving over the face of the waters. And God said (the voice of God is God the Son), "Let there be light."

After the creation of the Light, God (in Trinity) created the heavens, the earth, the moon, sun, and stars, the plants, and the animals. At every stage of the creation, God looked upon what He created "and saw that it was good. (Gen. 1: 4, 12, 18, 25)"

On the *"sixth day,"* God said *"Let us make man in Our image, after Our likeness . . . So God created man in His own image, in the image of God He created him; male and female He created them* (Gen. 1:26–27)." And after creating the man, God looked on what He created and saw that is was VERY good, the only time that this superlative is used in reference to the creation.

God gave man the Garden of Eden, where he lived in a state of Paradise. However, God gave the man free will. He did not force man to live in union with God. He gave him a choice. He told man, "*You may freely eat of every tree of the garden; but of the tree of the knowledge of good and evil you shall not eat, for in the day that you eat of it you shall die* (Gen. 2:16)."

But man was not content. Instead of feeling thankfulness for all that God had given to him, man was ungrateful. And tempted to eat from the tree, he did so. And God cast mankind out of Paradise, out from the Garden of Eden. Instead of living in unity with God, the human being now lived in a state of chaos—victim of his own mistakes, victim of the mistakes of others, and victim of a broken creation filled with "natural" (in reality unnatural, because God made nature perfect) disasters, until the day that each human being dies, and returns to the dust from which he was created.

A *wall of separation* separated man from God. In Genesis 3:24, we read, "God drove out the man; and at the east of the garden of Eden He placed the cherubim, and a flaming sword which turned every way, to guard the way to the tree of life."

God did not abandon His people though. He made a covenant with Noah (Gen. 9:13–17) that He would never destroy the earth with a flood again. He made a covenant with Abraham (Gen. 15) that God would be a Father to Abraham and all of His descendants. The sign of the covenant was circumcision (Gen. 17). God gave deliverance from famine through Joseph (Gen. 41). He gave deliverance to His people, the Israelites, from the oppression of Pharaoh (Exod. 14). God gave order to the people of Israel through the Ten Commandments (Exod. 20). He gave His people judges, kings and prophets in every generation, to let them know that they were not forgotten by Him. Throughout the Old Testament, there are prophecies foretelling of the coming of Christ the Messiah, who will save His people from their sins. *"But when the time had fully come, God sent forth His Son to redeem those under the Law* (Gal. 4:4)." This is the Feast of the Nativity. The story of the Nativity is told in Prophecy (Old Testament), the Gospels (New Testament), the Epistles (New Testament), and hymns and prayers (from the liturgical tradition). All will be used on our journey to the Nativity.

As we begin our journey, remember these three things—God made us in His image and likeness; we fell through sin; and through the Incarnation (which begins the earthly ministry of Christ that culminates in His Passion and Resurrection from the dead), we are reunited with Christ, as the Creator comes to live among His creation and redeem us from our sins.

Today's prayer is a hymn from the Vespers of Christmas, which tells us that through the Nativity the wall of separation between us and God came down.

> Come, let us rejoice in the Lord, as we tell about this mystery. The middle wall of separation has been broken down; the fiery sword has turned back, the Cherubim permits access to the tree of life; and I partake of the delight of Paradise, from which I was cast out because of disobedience. For the exact Image of the Father, the express Image of His eternity, take the form of a servant, coming forth form a Virgin Mother; and He undergoes no change. He remained what He was, true God; and He took up what He was not, becoming human in His love for humanity. Let us cry out to Him: "You who were born from a Virgin, O God, have mercy on us." (Trans. Fr. Seraphim Dedes.)

May God bless us as we take this journey together!

November 15

I am the Handmaiden of the Lord

*Now the birth of Jesus Christ took place in this way. When **His mother Mary** had been betrothed to Joseph, before they came together, she was found to be with child of the Holy Spirit.*
—Matthew 1:18

God's grand plan for our salvation involved incarnating the Word of God into the flesh, for God to become like one of us. And this would happen in a way that was both miraculous and understandable. The understandable part was that He would come into the world as a newborn baby. The miraculous part was that the conception would be by the Holy Spirit, an immaculate conception. A woman would bear God's Son in her womb and give birth to Him. So, God would bring His Son into the world through one of us.

The Virgin Mary was the woman that God selected for this task. She was born in a miraculous way to elderly parents named Joachim and Anna. When she was three years old, she was taken to the temple by her parents and given to the service of the Lord. After being raised in the temple for ten years, she found herself living in a small town called Nazareth, where she was betrothed (engaged) to a man named Joseph.

Historically, we believe that Mary was about fourteen when she was visited by the Archangel Gabriel. He greeted her with the words:

"Hail, O Favored Son, the Lord is with you! Behold, you
will conceive in your womb and bear a son, and you shall
call His name Jesus . . . The Holy Spirit will come upon
you, and the power of the most high will overshadow you;
therefore the child to be born will be called holy, the Son
of God." (Luke 1:28–35)

Can you imagine being in Mary's shoes? Visited by an angel? Told you
were going to do something that no one would believe?

Would you run? Would you doubt? Would you answer with
confidence?

Mary answered "Behold I am the handmaiden of the Lord; let it be to
me according to your word (Luke 1:38)." We don't know if Mary answered
with fear or with confidence. What we know is that she answered the call
of God. The other thing we know is God's plan for salvation couldn't have
come about if she hadn't answered "Yes!"

The lessons we learn from Mary are two: First, God calls everyone to
something in their life. There is no one who is uncalled. Some are called to
a certain vocation, or to be parents, some are called to serve in the military,
or to uproot their lives and move somewhere. Have you heard God's call
for your life? Have you answered? How have you answered?

The second lesson we learn is that just as Mary was part of God's plan
for our salvation, we, too, are part of God's plan for our own salvation.
God has provided the path to salvation. He has even provided the means
to go down the path—the church, the scriptures, the clergy, etc. But we
have to walk down the path ourselves. We work in concert with God in
order to attain salvation.

Mary is the model of what we are supposed to be! Because she said *yes* to the call of God. May we follow her example! Mary is called *Theotokos*, meaning, "God-bearer." We are called to be the same!

> O Virgin Theotokos who gave birth to the Savior, you reversed the curse to which Eve once was subject. For you have become the Mother of the Father's good pleasure, and you hold in your embraces God the Logos incarnate. The mystery admits to inquiry; we all glorify it by faith alone, and with you we cry aloud and say "O Lord incomprehensible, glory to You." (From the Praises, in the Orthros of the Nativity. Trans. Fr. Seraphim Dedes.)

May we strive to be servants today!

November 16

Ordinary People, Extraordinary Faith

*And her husband **Joseph, being a just man** and unwilling to put her to shame, resolved to divorce her quietly. But as he considered this, behold, an angel of the Lord appeared to him in a dream, saying "Joseph, son of David, do not fear to take Mary your wife, for that which is conceived in her is of the Holy Spirit; she will bear a son, and you shall call His name Jesus, for He will save His people from their sins."*
—Matthew 1:19–21

Joseph played an important role in the story as well. He was a rather ordinary man who had extraordinary faith. In Orthodox Tradition, we hold that Joseph was an elderly man, who had been widowed. He had children from a previous marriage, who are later referred to as Jesus's brothers and sisters who in reality were half-brothers and half-sisters (see Matt. 13: 55–56). Joseph worked as a carpenter—a rather ordinary life.

Joseph was a just man and the Gospel tells us that he did not want to put Mary to shame, so he resolved to divorce her quietly.

> But as he considered this, behold and angel of the Lord appeared to him in a dream saying, "Joseph, son of David, do not fear to make Mary your wife, for that which is conceived in her is of the Holy Spirit; she will bear a son and

you shall call His name Jesus, for He will save his people from their sins." (Matt. 1: 20–22)

We are told that "*when Joseph woke from sleep, he did as the angel of the Lord commanded him; he took his wife but knew her not until she had borne a son; and he called his name Jesus*" (Matt. 1:24–25).

Joseph had extraordinary faith. Imagine the conversation when Mary told him that she was pregnant. Here she had been raised in the temple. They were engaged, but not married. And now his betrothed was pregnant and the baby was not his. What faith he must have had in Mary, to believe that she was pregnant in a way no human being could become pregnant, by the Holy Spirit. And what faith he must have had in God to assume the role of caretaker for an unmarried woman who risked being scorned by the society of the day. He had the same risk as well. He had a job, he had friends, he had a reputation, and all those things he was willing to put on the line because of his faith.

There are two lessons from the life of Joseph. First, one can be a rather ordinary person and still make an extraordinary spiritual contribution. Joseph was not a priest, was not really learned (he had a trade, not a career), was not a member of the temple elite. He wasn't looking to play a big role when God tapped him on the shoulder. Yet, he, like Mary, embraced his role. You don't have to have a lot of money, or fame or a great career in order to answer God's call for your life. And secondly, Joseph was willing to risk his comfort, his job, his friends and so much more in order to care for Mary and her (not his) unborn child. Are we willing to do the same? Joseph's "Yes" to God was for a different thing than Mary. But it was really no less important. Because the story could not be complete without both of them.

An extraordinary person with little faith is rather ordinary in the eyes of God. An ordinary person with extraordinary faith, is extraordinary in the eyes of God. What kind of faith do you have? What kind of faith do you want to have? If you were standing in the presence of God right now, how would HE describe your faith?

> Tell us, o Joseph, how is it that you bring to Bethlehem great with Child the Maiden whom from the sanctuary you received? I, says he, have searched the Prophets and received a revelation from an Angel; and convinced am I that Mary shall give birth to God in ways surpassing all interpretation. And to worship Him shall Magi from the east come with precious gifts to pay homage unto Him. O Lord who for our sake have taken flesh, glory to You. (From the Royal Hours of the Nativity. Trans. Fr. Seraphim Dedes)

Be extraordinary in your faith today!

November 17

God is with Us

*All this took place to fulfill what the Lord had spoken by the prophet: Behold a Virgin shall conceive and bear a Son and **His name shall be called Emmanuel, which means God with us.** When Joseph woke from sleep, he did as the angel of the Lord commanded him; he took his wife but knew her not until she had borne a Son; and he called His name Jesus.*
—Matthew 1:22–25

It's amazing how much power there is in three simple words: "God with us." *God*—All powerful, provider, Comforter, Creator. *With*—wherever we go, He is there. On the busy road, in the doctor's office, in moments of triumph, in times of despair, God does not abandon His people. He is very much with us. *Us*—All people. God does not discriminate who can follow Him. His judgment only will come on those who don't.

Have you ever had a moment when you felt God with you? When you felt like His hand was right upon you? It doesn't happen often for me, but it has happened. And the times it has happened is when I was striving to walk WITH God—I can recall times of extremely fervent prayer, times of extreme humility and times of extreme. When I've laid it all on the line, so to speak, I have felt the presence of God. There are times when I hoped to feel the presence of God, but my own self got in the way. Holding back through lack of trust, or pushing myself forward with ego, these are the times that I feel God has been far away.

God desires to walk with us. Do we desire to walk with Him? Do we leave room for God to take up abode in us? Feeling God's presence "with us" really comes from how we perceive God's role in our life. For instance, if we feel that our body is ours and that our life is ours, and we fit God into a compartment, then He is like a tenant. We don't have a stake in Him. And even though He has a stake in us, it is hard to feel that when we are the owner and He is the tenant. When we see God as the owner of our body and the Lord of our life, then we see ourselves as tenants with the Lord as the over-arching landlord. Thus, we live for Him, and not for ourselves. And this is when we most acutely feel Him "with us."

I love what St. Paul writes in Romans 8:31–32: "What then shall we say to this? If God is for us, who is against us? He who did not spare His own Son but gave Him up for us all, will He not also give us all things with Him?"

And in II Corinthians, he writes,

> But as servants of God we commend ourselves in every way: through great endurance, in afflictions, hardships, calamities, beatings, imprisonments, tumults, labors, watching, hunger; by purity, knowledge, forbearance, kindness, the Holy Spirit, genuine love, truthful speech, and the power of God; with the weapons of righteousness for the right hand and for the left; in honor and dishonor, in ill repute and good repute. We are treated as imposters, and yet are true; as unknown, and yet well known; as dying, and behold we live; as punished, and yet not killed; as sorrowful, yet always rejoicing; as poor, yet making

many rich; as having nothing, and yet possessing every-thing. (II Cor. 6:4–10)

The lesson that St. Paul is teaching us is very simple. If God is with us, we can have nothing and yet still possess everything. Without God, however, we can have "everything" and yet still be accounted as nothing. God is with us! Are we with Him?

Be still, and know that I am God. I am exalted among the nations, I am exalted in the earth! The Lord of hosts is with us; the God of Jacob is our refuge. Psalm 46:10–11 (Read at the Royal Hours of the Nativity)

Go with God today!

November 18

We All Come from Somewhere

*In those days a decree went out from Caesar Augustus that all the world should be enrolled. This was the first enrollment, when Quirinius was governor of Syria. And all went to be enrolled, each to his own city. And Joseph also went up from Galilee, from the city of Nazareth, to Judea, to the city of David, which is called Bethlehem, because **he was of the house and lineage of David**, to be enrolled with Mary, his betrothed, who was with child.*
—Luke 2:1–5

On the Sunday before Christmas each year, the Gospel lesson is taken from Matthew 1, and includes the reading of forty-two generations between Abraham and Christ. Matthew's genealogy goes from Abraham to Christ. The Gospel of Luke, in Chapter 3, also includes the ancestors of Christ. There are more generations—seventy-six—and Luke counts the generations backward from Christ all the way back to Adam. Both lines include Abraham, Isaac, Jacob, David, etc. There are historical, cultural and social reasons for the divergence of number. The purpose of today's reflection is not to examine these generations in detail or account for their differences.

As they say, we all come from somewhere, and even Jesus came from earthly ancestry. They also say we can't pick our ancestors. Who they were and what they did are permanent, unchosen parts of who we are and where we come from. The lesson of the genealogy of Christ is that there were lots of different kinds of people in His earthly family. Some were trusting, like Abraham, who took his family and his possessions and moved because God told him to.

Isaac, his son, was tricked into giving away the birthright of his eldest son to his younger son Jacob. Jacob was sneaky. He also had two wives. Salmon, who begat Boaz, did so by Rahab, who had been a prostitute. And Boaz, who begot Obed, did so through Ruth, a Gentile, in a union that would not have been favored by the society of the day. David, the King and the Psalmist, who is seen as a righteous figure on balance, also had a dark side—He seduced Bathsheba, ordered his soldiers to kill Uriah, and his son Absalom died in young age. Jechoniah was held captive for thirty-seven years. And virtually nothing is known about Azor, Zadok, Achim, Eliud, Eleazar, Matthan, and Jacob.

In the ancestry of Christ, there were some memorable people and some forgettable ones. Some lived virtuous lives and many were far from virtuous. And there is hope and comfort in this. If Jesus Christ was descended through a line of spotless and mighty people, it would be hard to see Him as one of us, or taking on our burdens. We've all got some questionable ancestors in our past, and so does the Lord. We've also all got questionable deeds in our past. No one is perfect. Just because we have people we might wish were not part of our family tree or because we have things we've done that we wish were not part of our past, does not mean we can't live successfully, or grow spiritually. If the Messiah can come through a lineage of these kind of characters, well, he won't hold it against us if there are some characters who made some mistakes in our past, or if we ourselves, have made mistakes in our past.

Christianity, however, is not about where you've come from. It's about where you are and where you are going. If you have come, let's say, from a perfect line of ancestors, God is still going to judge you on your life, and not theirs. Knowing where you come from is important, when it comes to understanding who you are. And one other note on genealogies. It is up to each generation to sow the seed of faith into the ensuing generation. If you are reading this message and you are a Christian, you have an obligation, a sacred obligation, to make sure the line of Christianity doesn't stop at your generation. Every generation has the obligation—and the joy—to pass the Gospel to the generation that follows.

> Zion, the holy city of God, lift up your voices, truly heralding the divine, memorial of the Fathers, as you pay honor to them, Abraham and Isaac, with Jacob the acclaimed. With Judah and Levi, behold we now also magnify Moses the great one, along with Aaron the God-inspired, and we honor David and Joshua and Samuel. All of us striking up divine and sacred forefestal hymns in praise of Christ, are in earnest entreating Him that we may obtain the gift of His goodness that derives from Him who grants His great mercy to the world. (From the Praises of the Orthros of the Sunday before the Nativity. Trans. Fr. Seraphim Dedes.)

Have a great day!

November 19

His Purpose is Clear

And while they were there, the time came for her to be delivered. And she gave birth to her first born Son and **wrapped Him in swaddling clothes and laid Him in a manger** *because there was no place for them in the inn.*
—*Luke 2:6–7*

 f you look closely at many icons of the Nativity, you will notice that the manger is not a straw-filled wooden trough as we see in most Nativity displays around town. Rather, it resembles a casket or tiny tomb. The swaddling bands are not like the large cloth that we swaddle our children with, but rather are the burial bands used to bind the bodies of the dead. Why do the icons depict this? To make clear from the beginning the purpose of the Incarnation of Christ. His purpose in coming to be among us was to die for our sins. It all leads to the Cross and the Tomb. This is the reason Christ came to earth. This is the reason God incarnated His Only Begotten Son.

When you enroll in high school or college, what year do they label your class? It's the year you are scheduled to graduate. I entered college in 1990. I went in as the class of 1994, which ended up being the year I finished. Why do schools label classes by the year they finish, rather than the year they start? Because when you go to school, the purpose for your attendance is in order to finish. So, even from the first day of school, the focus is on the last. Sure, the journey is long, and fun, and important, but the focus of the journey is its end, not the journey itself, certainly not the beginning of it.

Our Christian life is the same. God's purpose in putting us here is so we can GRADUATE from this life, into eternal life. No one can get to heaven if they haven't lived on earth. Just like no one can graduate from college if they never spend a day in school. So, every day of our life, there should be a thought given to eternal life. This is why we hear at every Divine Liturgy (and in the daily vespers), a petition that speaks to us of "A Christian end to our lives, peaceful, without shame and suffering, and a good defense before the awesome judgment seat of Christ," so that this thought of our destination inspires how we spend our present journey.

Take some time every day, whether it is Christmas, or Advent, or the middle of summer, to work on your salvation, think about where you are headed for eternal life. So many people plan for retirement, but not for eternity. Spend time each day through prayer, meditation on scripture, obedience to the commandments and charity towards others. Spend a lifetime doing that and you will be in good shape for that accounting at the awesome judgment seat of Christ.

The Resurrection couldn't happen without the Nativity. However, the Nativity without the Resurrection would make Christ into an incredible teacher and healer, but not our Savior. An incredible life without Christ is just that—an incredible life that will one day come to an end. A life with Christ and a life in Christ is like going to school; you will be there for a while, you will even make good memories and have good times, but one day you will graduate to something bigger and better.

The purpose of Christ's Incarnation is apparent from the Nativity. God's purpose for our life is apparent from our birth as well!

Before Your birth, O Lord, the hosts of angels already perceived the mystery. They were struck with wonder and trembled, for though You adorn the heavens with stars, You are now well-pleased to be born as a Babe. You hold the ends of the earth in Your hands, but now You are laid in a manger of dumb beasts. Yet all these things fulfilled Your saving plan, by which Your compassion was revealed to us. Christ of great mercy, glory to You! (From the Royal Hours of the Nativity. Trans. Fr. Seraphim Dedes.)

Have a purposeful day!

November 20

It Was a Cave, Not a Barn!

And she gave birth to her first born Son and wrapped Him in swaddling clothes
*and **laid Him in a manger** because there was no place for them in the inn.*
—Luke 2:7

Every Nativity play I have ever watched has a scene where Mary and
Joseph go to an inn and are told that there are no rooms available.
They are, however, told that there is a stable out back and are shown to a
barn where the animals are kept, where Jesus is born and laid in a manger.
Every Nativity scene appearing under every Christmas tree shows a barn
with a straw roof and wooden walls with Jesus laying in a manger.

Yet every Orthodox icon shows Jesus Christ incarnate in a cave, in
the desert, outside of Bethlehem. Why a cave? Why not the traditionally
depicted barn or stable?

We are not told in scripture whether the birth took place in a barn or
a cave, only that there was no room in the inn. There are two reasons that
a cave is shown in Orthodox icons, rather than a barn. The first is actually
historical. At the time of the Nativity, animals were not kept sheltered in
wooden barns, but in caves and recesses in the hills. The second is sym-
bolic—the cave that is shown in the icons is traditionally surrounded by
sharp and steep rocks, which represent the cruel world into which Jesus
was Incarnate. The space inside the cave looks peaceful and welcoming.
The cave represents heaven. It is a peaceful respite from the world.

There is an icon that shows the cave, with the manger and the baby Jesus, with just the animals surrounding the manger and the star overhead. The theme of this icon is "*Creation worships the Creator.*" The significance of the feast of the Nativity is that the Creator came to live with His creation. Not only was there no room at any inn, but there was no room in any place made by human hands to hold the Creator of those hands. So, the Creator came to be part of His creation in a cave He Himself created.

In the last reflection, it was mentioned that in icons, the manger is depicted symbolically as a tomb. Historically, the manger was the wooden trough from where the animals were eating. Most likely it would have been filled with hay, which horses were eating. Again, there was no bed made by human beings that could hold the Creator. So, He was laid on straw, in wood that He created. His birth also reflects the most humble of beginnings. And it begins a ministry where Jesus would tell His followers: "Whoever would be great among you must be your servant, and whoever would be first among you must be slave of all. For the Son of man also came not to be served but to serve (Mark 10:43–45)."

The cave reflects peace, surrounded by danger. The manger shows humility. Later on, when we discuss how all of creation worshipped and brought gifts to the Creator in its midst, we will note that the earth itself worshipped the Creator, and for a gift, the earth offered a cave.

For today, examine peace and humility in your life. Does your life favor what is grandiose or simple? Are you more boastful or humble? If the cave reflects peace surrounded by danger, are you able to find inner peace in a life that is continually dangerous? Or have you succumbed to the dangers of the world? Today's verse is an important reminder of what is truly important—the virtues of peace and humility will go a long way in helping you grow as a Christian this Advent and far beyond it.

Today's hymn comes from a set of Katavasias (seasonal hymns in the Orthros service) which will be sung from November 21 through December 25. It references the mystery of the Nativity, noting the cave (which the translator has translated as "grotto" but in the Greek language appears as "*spileon*" which is usually translated as "cave"). These Katavasias begin with the bold announcement, "Christ is born, glorify Him!" and end with this hymn. Tomorrow on the Liturgical calendar, as the church celebrates the feast of the Entrance of the Virgin Mary into the temple, we will hear this announcement during the service for the first time this liturgical year, the announcement that the journey to the manger has begun.

> I see here a strange and paradoxical mystery. For, behold, the grotto is heaven; cherubic throne is the Virgin; the manger a grand space in which Christ our God the uncontainable reclined as a babe; Whom in extolling do we magnify. (Katavasias of the Nativity. Trans. Fr. Seraphim Dedes)

May your cave (your home, your work, your space) have peace today!

November 21

Is There Room in Your Inn?

And she gave birth to her first born Son and wrapped Him in swaddling clothes
*and laid Him in a manger because **there was no place for them in the inn.***
—Luke 2:7

In the Mexican culture, there is a Christmas-time tradition called Las Posadas. In this tradition, a couple dressed up as Mary and Joseph go from home to home, asking if there is any room at "the inn." Each home takes on the role of an inn in Bethlehem. They are rebuffed each time until they reach the home that has been designated as "the inn," at which point they are allowed in and a celebration ensues.

Imagine your heart as an inn—there are lots of rooms in it as there would be at an inn. At many inns, there are economy rooms, rooms with a view, rooms with a balcony, perhaps even a penthouse, or top floor room. Some rooms are more expensive and more lavish, others simpler.

The inn of your heart is similar. There are things in life, like relationships or family, that tug at our heart strings, and they often get the biggest rooms at the inn of our hearts. Careers get large rooms as well. Material possessions occupy space and so do our friends. Hobbies and things that bring us joy have a place, perhaps a smaller room, but there is still a place for them. Friday nights out with friends, Saturdays in front of the TV watching sports, the Sunday afternoon barbecue, they all find accommodations. Hopefully one's heart is big enough that there is a room for charity.

The question for today is which room does the Lord get in your heart? Is it the biggest one? Or the economy room? Is there a room for prayer? Worship? Charity? Are these rooms well-kept or in need of a remodel?

In the Nativity story, a woman who was about to deliver a child, and her betrothed, went from inn to inn, asking for lodging and help. There was no room in *any* inn. But even more poignant, there was no room in anyone's heart to extend charity and help to a woman at her moment of delivery. How could a city so filled with people not have had even one room, even one bit of charity for someone in need? Never mind that this woman was not just anyone, but God's chosen vessel for our salvation.

If your heart or your life is like an inn in Bethlehem, is there room in your inn for the Lord, or have all the spaces been filled with other things? In order to have Christ in your life, there needs to be not only room in "your inn," but the committed Christian offers Christ the best room, the first portion, of your life. The committed Christian has a room for charity, for prayer, for scripture reading, for obedience to the commandments. As we journey through Advent and prepare to celebrate the Nativity, it is a good time to clean the rooms of your heart and of your life, to make sure there is room for Christ in them.

Because just as they do at Las Posadas in Mexico, Christ comes to knock on the door of your heart every day. Do we turn Him away, saying there is no room at the inn, that all the rooms have been filled with other "things?" Or do we welcome Him with joy? Do we give Him the economy room? Or do we give Him the biggest and the best? Spend some time today evaluating how you spend your time. And reflect seriously on which rooms Christ occupies in the inn of your heart. Just like they upgrade rooms at hotels for special guests, consider giving an upgrade in your heart to Christ, the most special guest of all.

Gladsome light of the holy glory of the holy, blessed, heavenly, immortal Father, O Jesus Christ: arriving at the hour of sunset and having seen the evening light, we praise the Father, Son and Holy Spirit, God. It is worthy for You to be praised at all times with happy voices, O Son of God and Giver of life; and therefore the world glorifies You. (Vespers Hymn)

Open the door to your inn for Christ today!

November 22

The Message Is for Everyone

And in that region there were shepherds out in the field
keeping watch over their flocks by night.
—Luke 2:8

I'm sure during the period of the census in Bethlehem, there were people from all walks of life, all economic classes. There were well-to-do people who got the most expensive rooms in the most expensive inns, who rode the best donkeys and camels. With so many people descending on Bethlehem for the census, there were undoubtedly parties and family gatherings, reunions of friends, loud music, dancing and good food.

The shepherds were among the poorest of the people. They were not part of the Bethlehem social scene. Their work was done around the clock, in anonymity, with little compensation. I'm sure very few parents of the time dreamed for their children to be shepherds.

Yet, God chose "poor shepherds"List (the First Noel) to hear the good news. He chose to bless the shepherds to hear a multitude of the heavenly angels singing God's praises. And when the Shepherds told people what they had heard and seen, in a sense, He chose them to become the first evangelists, the first to share the good news.

Why these Shepherds? First, the message of Christ is for all people. He didn't take it to the high and mighty, but to the lowly. Christ's Nativity inaugurated the Kingdom of Heaven on earth, but He reigns with humility.

The message was given first to the most humble of people, simple shepherds. This is good news indeed, because the message of Christ IS for everyone. That includes not only every socioeconomic level; it includes every spiritual level:

If you've memorized the Christmas story, or can't remember most of the details, Christ's message is for you.

If you read the Bible every day, or have never read it before, Christ's message is for you!

If you pray every day, or if you've never said a genuine prayer, Christ's message is for you!

If Christ is the focus of your life, or if you are just starting your relationship with Him, Christ's message is for you!

Ok, so what is the message? The answer comes from the shepherds as well. One of the ways Christ reveals Himself is as "the Good Shepherd." In John 10: 11–15, we read:

> Jesus said, "I am the Good Shepherd. The Good Shepherd lays down His life for the sheep. He who is a hireling and not a shepherd, whose own the sheep are not, sees the wolf coming and leaves the sheep and flees; and the wolf snatches them and scatters them. He flees because he is a hireling and cares nothing for the sheep. I am the Good Shepherd; I know My own and My own know Me, as the Father knows Me and I know the Father; and I lay down My life for the sheep."

Jesus uses this image because all Christians are like a flock of sheep. Jesus is our Shepherd. Jesus protects the flock from "wolves" and all harm. When one sheep is lost, like a good shepherd, He goes in search of the lost sheep. Most important, like a good shepherd keeps his flock together until they get safely to their pen at the end of the day, Jesus keeps His flock together and provides for our safety until we reach the permanent safety of heaven at the end of our lives.

I hope that the images sticking in your mind are not the loud and raucous parties of Bethlehem, but the peace of the cave and the safety of the pen. For many people, if you asked them where they want to end up—a cave, a pen, or a party—the answer most certainly would be the party. The message of Christ is that we want to end up in the cave and safely in the pen. It is in humility that we experience Christ. The message is for everyone!

> Give ear to my words, o Lord; give heed to my groaning.
> Hearken to the sound of my cry, my King and my God,
> for to Thee do I pray. O Lord, in the morning Thou dost
> hear my voice; in the morning I prepare a sacrifice for
> Thee and watch . . . But I through the abundance of Thy
> steadfast love will enter Thy house, I will worship toward
> Thy holy temple in the fear of Thee. Lead me, O Lord in
> Thy righteousness because of my enemies; make Thy way
> straight before me. (Ps. 5:1–3, 7–8. (Read at the Royal
> Hours of the Nativity)

Be witness for Christ to everyone you meet today!

November 23

Bethlehem Was Too Busy to Notice

*And in that region there were shepherds **out in the field***
keeping watch over their flocks by night.
—Luke 2:8

We've all experienced the stress of the mall at Christmas. Fighting over parking places, waiting in traffic, and long lines in the stores, and now added to that everyone looking at their phone, WHILE fighting for parking, sitting in traffic and waiting in line. I remember once thinking, with all of this stress at the mall, would anyone even notice if a multitude of angels appeared over the mall? The glory of the Lord over the mall of your town might actually go unnoticed.

It's no wonder that the message came to shepherds out in a field. They were the only ones who weren't overstimulated. Think about it—has God ever revealed Himself to you while you were stuck in traffic? It's never happened to me. God reveals Himself when we are open to receiving Him. That's why I've never experienced God in a traffic jam, or with the radio blaring, or at a crowded stadium. I experience God most powerfully in prayer, in worship, and sometimes even in conversation with one other person. Notice how I said "with one other person." I have felt God's powerful presence when hearing confession and when offering my own confession. I have felt God more strongly with two people in church than with two hundred. I have experienced God in silence more than I ever have when there is lots of noise.

I'm reminded of the story of the small, still voice that Elijah heard the Lord in. In I Kings 19:9–13, we read:

> And there he (Elijah) came to a cave, and lodged there; and behold, the word of the Lord came to him and He said to him, "What are you doing here, Elijah?" He said, "I have been very jealous for the Lord, the God of hosts; for the people of Israel have forsaken Thy covenant, thrown down Thy altars and slain Thy prophets with the sword; and I, even I only, am left; and they seek my life, to take it away." And he said "Go forth, and stand upon the mount before the Lord." And behold, the Lord passed by, and a great and strong wind rent the mountains, and broke in pieces the rocks before the Lord, but the Lord was not in the wind; and after the wind an earthquake, but the Lord was not in the earthquake; and after the earthquake a fire, but the Lord was not in the fire; and after the fire a still small voice. And when Elijah heard it, he wrapped his face in his mantle and went out and stood at the entrance of the cave. And behold, there came a voice to him.

No, it wasn't at the mall of Bethlehem where the good news was announced. It was in the quiet of the countryside, to the shepherds quietly going about their work. If you want to feel closer to Christ, turn off some of the noise. Put down the phone, get off email, stay away from the mall, and get on your knees and pray, read the scriptures, and listen for the small, still voice of God. Everyone is busy, but there is no one too busy for God.

Certainly God isn't ever too busy to hear our prayers. Even the shepherds were busy tending to their flocks. They weren't doing nothing. Take some strides so that your life resembles the quiet hillside outside of Bethlehem rather than the chaos on the Bethlehem streets. Work was being done on both of them for sure. The glory of the Lord appeared all over that region. On the busy streets of Bethlehem, it was somehow missed. On the quiet hillside, it wasn't.

> On this day the Virgin Maid goes to the grotto to give birth to the Pre-Eternal Word in an ineffable manner. Dance for joy, all the inhabited earth, on hearing. Glorify along with Angels and with the shepherds Him who will that He appear as a newborn Child, the pre-eternal God. (Kontakion of Advent. Trans. Fr. Seraphim Dedes)

Leave room for God in your schedule today!

Watching Your Flock Isn't Always Glamorous

*And in that region there were shepherds out in the field **keeping watch over their flocks by night**.*
—Luke 2:8

*B*eing a shepherd was certainly not a glamorous job. It involved herding a large number of sheep to go into a specific direction. Of course, the sheep don't have the power of persuasion and reason that human beings have, so this was a tough task. Oftentimes the ratio of sheep could be 100 sheep to one shepherd. Predatory animals like wolves often attacked the sheep, so in addition to keeping his sheep united, the shepherd also had to keep them safe. At night, the shepherd would station himself at the gate of the sheep pen where he could protect the doorway of the pen from predators. He had to sleep with one eye open it would seem, so as not to be caught by surprise. And because he had nothing but the moon and the stars for light, he had to be extra vigilant from an attack in the dark. Combine this with the changing seasons, some of those winter nights could be moonless, long and cold. Being a shepherd was a hard job.

Then you contrast the warmth of Bethlehem on the night of the Nativity with the cold of the countryside, and on top of suffering from fear and the elements, the shepherds also suffered from isolation. They knew what was going on in Bethlehem and knew they were excluded from it—but the shepherds were faithful. They didn't abandon their flocks. They didn't rise up in protest. The icons of the Nativity show the shepherds modeling patience and faithfulness to their task, difficult as it was.

Many times in church circles, a priest will refer to his congregation as his "*flock*." This seems appropriate, given the image of the Christians as sheep and the clergy, representing Christ, as the shepherds. When I was a young priest, I was entrusted with a small flock at a small parish. Having grown up in a large parish that was always filled with people on Sundays, and having served for one year as a Deacon to the Bishop of Boston where every service was celebrated in a full church, it was an adjustment to celebrate the liturgy with a "flock" of only a few people. I constantly thought of the day I'd get a larger flock, and was envious of priests that I thought had better flocks than I did.

Over time, however, I have learned to love the flock with which I have been entrusted, and I have learned to "keep watch over" the flock as best I can. On Christmas and Holy Week, that flock will number more people than I can count. On a Sunday, the flock fills the church. On a weekday service, the flock may be only a few. When someone comes for confession, I keep watch over a flock of one. I've learned that keeping watch over the flock means to give the best you can whether the flock numbers one or one hundred or one thousand. It also means to love the flock you have, rather than looking at other flocks around you and wishing you were THEIR shepherd.

Society puts so much pressure on people to be a certain thing, or look a certain way, or own certain possessions. Christmas shopping becomes a competition to keep up with the Joneses. Many people struggle with the same issue I struggled with years ago (and once in a while still struggle with)—they have a hard time embracing the flock that they have. Some people wish they had a different spouse, or more (or less) children, or a better job. The teacher wishes for a different class. The lawyer for a bigger client. The doctor for a patient that is going to get better. The coach for the better team. The business owner for more success. Many times we are so preoccupied with looking at other flocks that we don't nurture the flock that has been entrusted to us. So, if your flock is one child, a difficult class, a patient that isn't going to get better, a mediocre team, or a struggling business, watch over YOUR flock as best you can. For the Lord crowns not success, but effort. We can't always control success, but we can always control effort.

As I meditate on today's verse, my eye goes to the word "their." The shepherds were keeping watch over THEIR flocks by night. They weren't looking at the flocks of others. They weren't rebelling because they weren't in Bethlehem. They were making the best of what they had. So watch over your flock today—your family, your co-workers, your students, patients, and customers. Even when it gets dark and cold and monotonous, even when you are in the fields and others are in the city, watch over YOUR flock. For as we will read in the next reflection, it was not busy Bethlehem that saw the glory of the Lord, but the shepherds who were watching THEIR flocks.

> O Christ our God, who at all times and at every hour, both in heaven and on earth, are worshipped and glorified, long suffering and plenteous in mercy and compassion; who love the just and show mercy to the sinners; who call all men to salvation through the promise of the blessings to come: Do You, the same Lord, receive also our supplications at this present time, and direct our loves according to Your commandments. (Prayer of the

Hours, from the Royal Hours of the Nativity, Trans. Fr. Seraphim Dedes)

May God bless and protect you and your flock today!

November 25

The Glory of the Lord

*And an angel of the Lord appeared to them, and the **glory of the Lord**
shown around them, and they were filled with fear.*
—Luke 2:9

Have you ever thought about the word *glory*? Have you ever wondered what "the glory of the Lord" might look like?

In Exodus 33:18–23, God shows His glory to Moses:

> Moses said, "I pray Thee, show me Thy glory." And He
> [God] said, "I will make all my goodness pass before you,
> and will proclaim before you My name 'The Lord'; and I
> will be gracious to whom I will be gracious and will show
> mercy on whom I will show mercy. But," He said, "you
> cannot see My face; for man shall not see me and live."
> And the Lord said "Behold, there is a place by Me where
> you shall stand upon the rock; and while My glory passes
> by I will put you in a cleft of the rock, and I will cover
> you with My hand until I have passed by; then I will take
> away My hand, and you shall see my back; but My face
> shall not be seen."

And reading further, we see that Moses was profoundly impacted by the experience:

> When Moses came down from Mount Sinai, with the
> two tablets of the testimony in his hand as he came down
> from the mountain, Moses did not know that the skin
> of his face shone because he had been talking with God.
> And when Aaron and all the people of Israel saw Moses,
> behold, the skin of his face shone and they were afraid to
> come near him. (Exod. 34:29–30)

In the Gospels, we read about the Transfiguration of Christ, when He was Transfigured in glory before three of His disciples, "And He was transfigured before them, and His face shone like the sun, and His garments became white as light (Matt. 17:2)."

Imagine these poor shepherds watching their flocks by night, trying to fight off sleep and keep warm from the cold; all of a sudden an angel appears to them and the glory of the Lord surrounds them. A black sky is suddenly filled with light so bright that you can't look at it. Busy Bethlehem misses the miracle. It is experienced by the shepherds. How powerful it must have been for them to see God's glory!

Our modern definition of glory is quite different. Glory is used to describe accolades and other things for which one is given fame. For instance the hero of the Superbowl gets all the glory and fame that comes with winning the game.

Glory is also used to describe better days gone by. For instance, from 1963–1975, the UCLA men's basketball team won ten national titles including seven in a row. These years are known as the *glory years* of their program. Some of you may be old enough to remember them.

But here is the thing with these two definitions of glory—eventually they fade. Eventually everyone who remembers a Superbowl hero or the UCLA dynasty dies; and those stories of glory are only read about in magazines and watched in movies. Indeed man's "glory" is fleeting.

The glory of God is something that the faithful Christians will live in forever. God's glory never fades.

We get glimpses of God's glory in this life as well. We stand in His glory when we receive Communion. In the Eucharist, the human being touches the Divine God. We touch His glory. His glory shines on us. We stand in His glory when we offer a heartfelt prayer. We stand in His glory when we glorify Him in what we do, when we do something for Him. Two people who pray together share His glory.

And the glory of God changes people. Standing in the sunlight will change the color of your skin. Standing in the Light of Christ will change the color of your heart. If you want to feel God's glory, spend five minutes a day praying from now until the Nativity—thirty days—and watch how that will change your life. If you are someone who already does this, you know what I mean. Look upon the face of someone who has stood in God's glory and they don't look lost. They look at peace. They can even be stressed out and still be in peace. God's glory changes people. It allows them small glimpses into God's kingdom in this life. It prepares them to stand in God's glory for eternal life.

> May the glory of the Lord endure forever, may the Lord rejoice in His work, who looks on the earth and it trembles, who touches the mountains and they smoke! I will sing to the Lord as long as I live; I will sing praise to my God while I have being. May my meditation be pleasing to Him, for I will rejoice in the Lord. Let sinners be

consumed from the earth, and let the wicked be no more! Bless the Lord o my soul! Praise the Lord! (Ps. 104:31–35. Read at the Vespers of the Nativity)

Have a Glory-ous day!

November 26

Be Not Afraid

*And they were filled with fear. And the angel said to them, **"Be not afraid."***
—Luke 2:9–10

Think about when you are most afraid. It's when you don't know the outcome of something. People feel fear before they take a test, particularly medical tests, because they don't know what the outcome is going to be. People are afraid of the unknown, because they don't have mastery of it and can't control the results. People get afraid when they upset friends because they wonder if they've permanently damaged a relationship. Sometimes fear is irrational. For instance, I used to get very afraid during scary movies, until I realized that the people on the screen are just actors, and no one is really going to get hurt or die on the movie set. Most of the time, however, fear is real, and powerful, and even debilitating.

Imagine these shepherds working in the quiet, yet predictably hazardous conditions in the fields outside of Bethlehem. And then an angel appears, surrounded by God's glory. Naturally, the shepherds were afraid. After all, what is an angel? And what was surrounding the angel?

How would YOU feel is you were confronted by an angel? Would you be filled with fear, or joy? I'd have to say that I'd be filled with fear, at least until I understood the message and purpose of the angel's visit. The reaction of the shepherds was quite normal.

The first thing the angel says to the shepherds, *before* delivering the good news, ministers to their trepidation. The angel says, calmly and reassuringly, "Be not afraid." His tone is not judgmental but reassuring.

One of the wonderful things about God is that He reassures us. He invites us. In Matthew 11:28–30, Jesus tells us:

> Come to me, all who labor and are heavy laden, and I will give you rest. Take My yoke upon you, and learn from Me, for I am gentle and lowly in heart, and you will find rest for your souls. For My yoke is easy, and My burden is light.

What a great thought for those who are stressed out!

And in Luke 15:7, Jesus says, "There is more joy in heaven over one sinner who repents than over ninety-nine who need to repentance." What a comforting thought for the person who feels estranged from God because of his sins. You know how many people tell me that they feel far from God because of what they've done. I tell them, "come back to God, and when you do, the angels will be rejoicing in heaven. Just because your relationship with Christ isn't what it should be, there is no need to fear. There is great incentive to come back."

Psalm 103: 17-18 addresses fear by telling us, "But the steadfast love of the Lord is from everlasting to everlasting upon those who fear Him, and His righteousness to children's children, to those who keep His covenant and remember to do His commandments." Love from everlasting to everlasting, even to those who are afraid! There is no need to fear at all!

Now for a practical application: God reassures us; we have to reassure one another. Many times, whether we intend to or not, we PUT fear into our neighbor. Whether we intend to or not, at times we all cause the blood pressure of our neighbor to rise. There are people in my life that my palms sweat when I have to call them on the phone. They make me feel fear. So, one goal you should strive to have in your life is to have no one who is afraid of you. To have no one who feels they have to tip-toe on egg-shells because of you. When your neighbor is nervous, remember the words of God's angel: Be not afraid. We get the chance to play the role of the angel more often than we think—to our spouses, our children, our co-workers and our friends. Take every opportunity to reassure people.

How awesome is the mystery that was about to be revealed by the angel to the shepherds. Truly awesome are the mysteries of God. Holy Communion is a mystery—how bread and wine become the Body and Blood of Christ is a mystery. But the opportunity we have to receive these Gifts is truly AWEsome. It should fill us with AWE and a measure of fear. After all, we can't take the opportunity to touch the Divine lightly. A healthy fear and awe and respect is a good thing. We shouldn't have so much fear that we stay away from the things of God. We should have a healthy respect for the things of God so that we can maintain a sense of reverence as we partake of them, and self-control as we prepare to do so.

We naturally fear what we do not know. The shepherds had that fear. But listen to the message of God, told to us over and over again throughout the scriptures. His consistent message is "Be NOT afraid." And once we get over our fear, and replace fear with awe and respect, then we are more ready to hear the message which follows.

Do not be afraid to develop a relationship with God. Do not make others afraid to develop a relationship with you!

> Sanctify our souls; purify our bodies; set our minds right;
> clear up our thoughts, and deliver us from every sorrow,
> evil and distress. Surround us with Your holy Angels so
> that being guarded and guided by their presence we may

arrive at the unity of the faith and the knowledge of Your ineffable glory; for blessed are you unto the ages of ages. Amen. (Prayer of the Hours, from Royal Hours of the Nativity. Trans. Fr. Seraphim Dedes)

Have an AWEsome day!

November 27

What is the Good News?

*And the angel said to them, "Be not afraid, for I bring you **good news of a** **great joy** which will come to all the people."*
—*Luke 2:10*

What is the good news? In the Nativity story, the Angels gave the message, "For to you is born this day in the city of David, a Savior who is Christ the Lord (Luke 2:11)."

What does that mean to us?

Let's go back to Genesis and the Creation. In Genesis 2:7 we read, "Then the Lord God formed man of dust from the ground, and breathed into his nostrils the breath of life; and man became a living being." What God breathed into the human being was a soul. The body was taken from the dust of the ground, and given a soul. The human being is composed of mind, body and soul, with the soul being tied to the mind because we are rational beings. Only the human being has a soul, no other created entity has a soul. The soul is what makes us in the "image and likeness" of God (Gen. 1:26–27). Indeed this was good news.

Remember the first thing you need to believe to be a Christian—that God made us, and that He made us like Him. He made us perfect. He created us to live forever.

When mankind fell, through ingratitude and disobedience, God punished mankind. In Genesis 3:19, we read that God told man: "In the sweat of your face you shall eat bread till you return to the ground, for out of it you were taken; you are dust, and to dust you shall return."

This is sad news. To think that beautiful human beings, who are so filled with talent, were sharing a common destiny of being returned again to the earth after we die. And the God-like part of us, the soul, which will live forever, like God, suffered an even worse fate. For the soul, its life did not end with physical death. Rather the soul was consigned to Hades, to darkness, to live forever with the devil that deceived humanity into falling in the first place.

If you go back to your days of high-school algebra, we all learned how to balance an algebra equation. We did it by doing the same thing to both sides of the equation. Well, if you look at the Creation of the world like an algebra equation, when the human being was created in the image and likeness of God, you could say that the equation was balanced between God and man. Obviously man cannot be equal to God because God created man. The Fall unbalanced the equation, because now on man's side of the equation, there was hardship, disease, and ultimately death and a descent to Hades.

With the Incarnation, Christ came down to earth to balance the equation. He experienced all of the human experiences—He got hungry and wanted to eat from a fig tree (Matt. 21:18). He got tired and asked a woman at a well for water (John 4:6). He got angry at the moneychangers in the temple (John 2:15). He was afraid as He meditated on His own death (Matt. 26:39). He got sad, and wept at the tomb of His friend Lazarus (John 11:35).

Christ experienced a human death, and a painful one at that. He died on the cross. And in that moment, the equation was balanced, because now the Son of God had experienced the punishment of death given to the fallen humanity. Jesus also descended to Hades. But then He rose from the dead, ascended into heaven and sat at the right hand of the Father, with the "glory which I had with Thee before the world was made" (John 17:5).

When Jesus died on the cross, He expressed perfect faith in God when He said, "Father into Thy hands I commit my spirit (Luke 23:46)!" Our goal in life is to reach the end of life with this kind of perfect faith in God, demonstrated through our works, and then by His Grace, we too can be resurrected, ascend to heaven, and sit at the right hand of the Father. Once we get to heaven, the equation of us with God stays balanced forever, for we are told that heaven is permanent. Once one is there, he cannot fall out of heaven (Luke 16:26).

The good news for us is that despite our fallen nature, we can still become one with God. No one has to die a violent death in order to do this. We have to love God, and love our neighbor. We have to be kind, show mercy, forgive, all things that we are more than capable of doing. We have to believe and trust in God. These things are a little harder. But the good news is that we have our whole life to figure this out. The bad news is that we do not know how long that life will be.

Jesus expressed in His Prayer to God the Father, on behalf of humanity, that He offered in the Garden of Gethsemane before His Passion, what His hope was for all of us, when He prayed: "Father, I desire that they also, whom Thou hast given Me, may be with Me where I am, to behold My glory which Thou hast given Me in Thy love for Me before the foundation of the world (John 17:24)."

There you have the good news. Christ *wants* us to behold His glory and to be with Him in Paradise, the way Adam and Eve were before the Fall. *That* is what He wants for all of us. He has given us the path to get there. His Resurrection from the dead makes that possible. His incarnation makes the resurrection possible. What great news indeed!

Christ is born; therefore glorify! Christ is come from heaven; go and meet Him. Christ is on earth; arise to Him. Sing to the Lord, all you who dwell on the earth; and in merry spirits, O you people, praise His birth. For He is glorified. (Katavasias of the Nativity, Trans. Fr. Seraphim Dedes)

Have a great day!

November 28

What Is Joy?

*And the angel said to them, "Be not afraid, for I bring you good **news of a** **great joy** which will come to all the people."*
—Luke 2:10

What is joy? Have you ever stopped to think about the meaning of this word?

Joy is the feeling that a child has on Christmas morning when he or she tears the wrapping paper off of presents, not knowing what treasure lies inside but knowing they will like it. Joy is the anticipation as we arrive at the end of a journey and we're about to greet a friend we haven't seen in a long time. Joy is the warm embrace we exchange with a spouse or a child that never seems to get old no matter how often we do it.

This is the kind of joy that we are supposed to have about being a Christian. Tearing through the pages of the Bible, anticipating uncovering some great treasure like a child has on Christmas morning as he or she opens presents. We should have the same joyful anticipation that one feels at the end of a journey when we have made it through the journey of the week and are about to greet the Lord in church on Sunday mornings. That warm embrace that we never tire of, that is the feeling we should have when we pray. For in prayer we embrace God and He embraces us.

Why is it that we don't have more joy in the world? I mean, everywhere you turn people seem to be angry, cynical, or jaded. We are suspicious of one another instead of trusting. The idea of joy seems like an idea of an age gone by.

I remember one year when our son was a toddler, that we came back from a vacation and as we entered into our house, he ran into his room and grabbed all his toys as if they were all brand new. As I think back on his life, that was one of his most joyful days. So, we know there IS joy in the world, and it is found in our children. It is found in innocence, even in silliness.

The Bible makes a distinction between child-ish and child-like. Jesus says in Matthew 18:3, "Truly I say to you, unless you turn and become like children, you will never enter the kingdom of heaven." Jesus encourages us to be child-like.

St. Paul, on the other hand, warns us not to be child-ish, when he writes I Corinthians 13:11, "When I was a child, I spoke like a child, I thought like a child, I reasoned like a child; when I became a man, I gave up childish ways."

So, what is the difference between child-ish and child-like? Throwing a tantrum is childish. Pouting and crying is childish. Having to be told to do something twenty times is childish. These are things we should have left behind with our childhood years.

What about the joy of opening presents on Christmas morning?! What about the fun of playing a game? What about the ability to laugh easily and forgive quickly? These are things from our childhood that we should have in our adult life. Many people will scoff at the idea of playing a silly game; and yet a silly game provides the opportunity for pure laughter and unadulterated joy.

When we were children, we'd promise something by "crossing my heart and hope to die." Today we promise something by a lengthy contract. We'd play tag and no one minded when it was their turn to be "it." I can only imagine how an adult game of tag would go—endless arguments and appeals and probably a good measure of cheating thrown in as well.

The Christmas season hopefully helps to take us back to the joy of childhood. Putting up a Christmas tree, putting up ornaments, turning on the lights, opening presents should be acts of joy.

Being a Christian should bring us joy as well. I confess there are times when I am not especially looking forward to going to Liturgy, when my mind is on things other than the sacred task I am doing. But more often than not, I feel joy when I celebrate the Liturgy. My liturgical joy is a child-like joy. I usually can't wait to come, to pray, to worship. In the same way a child can watch a movie dozens of times and not get bored, I can offer the liturgy hundreds of times, and often many days in a row and still feel joy about it.

I confess that prayer is still more work than joy for me on many occasions; that is the thing I have to work on. I do know that when I pray a lot, it does bring joy; it's just a question of getting started.

Adding laughter and silliness to your life is a good thing. Of course, do it in a wholesome, Christian way. We shouldn't have fun or silliness by demeaning ourselves or someone else. Help create environments where it is okay for adults to be silly, whether it is a game night, or a comedy movie night, karaoke, there are lots of possibilities. When you pray, ask God to put a child's heart in you, so that like a child, you can forgive easily, so that like a child, you'll walk into church with a sense of wonder, which can then become joy. The news of the angel to the shepherds was not just "good news" but "good news of a great joy." As we prepare to hear the good news again, may we prepare our hearts to joyfully receive it.

Come, God-inspired faithful, arise and behold the descent of God form on high! He manifests Himself to us in Bethlehem! Let us cleanse our minds, and offer Him a life of virtue instead of myrrh. Let us prepare with faith to celebrate His Nativity, storing up spiritual treasure and crying: Glory in the highest to God in Trinity! His good pleasure is now revealed to men: As the Lover of mankind He sets Adam free from the ancestral curse. (Hymn from the Royal Hours of the Nativity. Trans. Fr. Seraphim Dedes)

Have a joyful day!

November 29

Sharing the Good News

And the angel said to them, "Be not afraid, for I bring you good news of a
*great joy **which will come to all the people.**"*
—*Luke 2:10*

Many years ago, when we lived in Connecticut, we hosted a priest from Africa (Uganda) for Christmas in our home. When I picked him up from his seminary dorm room on December 23, I saw that he didn't have much in the way of belongings. He told me that most of his property had been lost on the plane coming over from Africa the previous summer. I decided to take him to the mall to get some things, like a hot plate, a watch, a Bible—basic things that we all take for granted and he didn't have.

It turns out that he had never been to any store other than the CVS drugstore near the seminary and going to the mall was an overwhelming experience. We went into the Sears store, where we saw 100 TVs on one wall of the store. He exclaimed "I don't know if I've seen 100 TVs in my whole life and here I am seeing 100 of them at the same time." He watched everyone scurrying around doing their last minute shopping and asked me "why are these people so stressed out, Christmas is only a couple of days away, they should be filled with joy." I answered, "They are stressed out because they have been trying for months to find the perfect gifts for everyone on their lists and now they have only two days left." We spent some time shopping and some time people-watching. My friend shook his head, continuing to wonder how Christmas could be so stressful.

We came upon a long line of children, waiting to see Santa Claus. He asked me "What is this all about?" When I tried to explain the concept of Santa Claus he said, "That is ridiculous. Who could believe such a thing?" To which I answered "Every kid in America under age ten!" He wondered with what right kids go to Santa to demand what they expect for Christmas.

When Christmas came, we celebrated two beautiful liturgies in church. When it was time to open gifts, we had a present for him. It was a black sweater, a safe bet if you are looking for something to buy a priest. We told him, "If it doesn't fit, we can take it back and get you something else." He answered "You gave it to me, I will treasure it forever." After dinner, as we called our families for Christmas, we asked him if there was anyone he'd like to call. He said he hadn't heard from his parents in months, as their village was remote, and terrorist guerillas were always harming Christians. After a while, he came downstairs and was crying. He said he spoke to his parents and was so grateful they were still alive. He said this was the best Christmas present ever.

Father was enamored with Christmas lights. In fact, we bought him some lights which he later put up at the church in his village, the only place that had electricity.

That year, 1999, Christmas fell on a Saturday, so we went to church on Friday for Christmas Eve and Saturday for Christmas Day. We got up early and drove to church on Sunday, December 26, and as we drove down the main street of the town at 8:00 A.M. the morning after Christmas, we found it was bumper-to-bumper traffic. My priest-friend was excited. "What great Christians you have here in Connecticut!" he exclaimed. "They went to church on Friday for Christmas Eve and yesterday for

Christmas and today again!" I said "Father, the church will be empty today. All of these people are going back to the mall to take their gifts back." "What?" he asked. "Didn't you tell me that people spend months shopping for Christmas and now not even hours after Christmas is over they are taking their gifts back?!" That afternoon, we went for a walk around town and a man was throwing out his Christmas tree. My friend shouted to him "Merry Christmas!" The man answered him with a cold, "Christmas is over!" My friend said, "No, Christmas just started. I've fasted for forty days, and now I'm ready to celebrate."

I share this story for two reasons. First, because if you take a step back and look at how we've come to celebrate Christmas, we're getting it all wrong. Christmas is filled with stress instead of with joy. And once Christmas comes, instead of celebrating, we're relieved that it is over. We've commercialized Christmas—it is not a season of holiness but a season of advertising, sales and business transactions.

Second, as the angels told the shepherds, the good news of great joy is for all people. The Greek priest from middle-class America and the priest with dark skin from the remote village in Africa looked at Christmas differently. We came from different life experiences. We were far apart on an economic level. But where there was absolute unity was that we both love the Lord, and He loves both of us. We both believe in Him because He died for both of us. We both celebrated the Nativity in the same way, with joy and gratitude.

Our world is so obsessed with the concept of equality. Yet equality is a fallacy—no two people, no two days, no two of anything are equal. God places infinite value on each person. Rather than obsessing over where we stand as compared to our neighbor, we should always be cognizant of where we stand in the sight of God. He loves us with an infinite love. Is our gratitude just as infinite?

Indeed the good news is for all people—every race, every nation, every color, rich, poor, educated, illiterate, whether you've never opened the Bible or read it faithfully, whether you know God well or have never said a prayer—everyone one is invited to share in the Good News, and become an inheritor of God's heavenly kingdom. ALL are called. All are called to the manger!

> Listen, heaven! Give ear, O earth! Let the foundations of the earth be shaken! Let trembling seize the regions beneath the earth, for our God and Creator has clothed Himself in created flesh; He fashioned all creation, yet reveals Himself in the womb of her that He formed. O the depth of the riches of the wisdom and knowledge of God! How incomprehensible are His judgments; and how unsearchable His ways! (Hymn from the Royal Hours of the Nativity. Trans. Fr. Seraphim Dedes)

Have an infinitely blessed day!

November 30

Why Do I Need a Savior?

"For to you is born this day in the city of David,
a Savior *who is Christ the Lord"*
—Luke 2:11

Are you saved? We hear this question a lot in religious circles. What does it mean for us?

In order to be found, one has to have a sense that he or she is lost. And in order to be saved, one has to have a sense that he or she needs saving. The questions then are: What do I need saving from? And how am I saved?

Before answering these questions, allow me to redefine some terms we use in our society. We use the word "life" to refer to the period of time we are alive on earth. We use the word "death" to refer to the moment when life on earth ends. To understand salvation, it is helpful redefine these terms. Let's call our time on earth "preparation" because the time is temporary, and our time on earth prepares us for what comes after the time is over. "Passing" is what happens when preparation is over. We "pass away." And the opportunity to prepare ends. And then after we pass away, one of two things happens. Either we go to eternal LIFE which we call salvation in the Kingdom of Heaven, or we die, and are permanently estranged from God. We live in a state of death and eternal condemnation.

We prepare. We pass. And then we either go to life or to death.

To the question "from what are we being saved," the answer is that by living a life in Christ, we are saved from death. Jesus tells us in John 5:24, "Truly, truly I say to you, he who hears My word and believes Him who sent Me, has eternal life; he does not come into judgment, but has passed from death to life." We are all going to undergo a physical death, that is we will all stop breathing at some point, our bodies will shut down, and they will be buried and decay. Our souls will go to God for judgment and they will pass either into a state of condemnation, or into eternal life. Again, Jesus tells us in John 11:25–26, "I am the Resurrection and the Life; he who believes in Me, though he die, yet shall he live, and whoever lives and believes in Me shall never die." And in St. Paul's Epistle to the Romans, he writes: "Do you not know that all of us who have been baptized into Christ Jesus were baptized into His death? We were buried therefore with Him by baptism into death, so that as Christ was raised from the dead by the glory of the Father, we too might walk in newness of life. For if we have been united with Him in a death like His, we shall certainly be united with Him in a Resurrection like His (Rom. 6:3–5)."

We are saved from death, which is eternal separation from God, and through the death and Resurrection of Christ, we have a pathway to salvation, which is eternal life in the Kingdom of God.

How then are we saved? The simple answer is that we are not saved in ONE moment of time. Many Christians ascribe to the teaching of "once saved, always saved," so that if a person comes forth at a specific moment in time, they can say "I was saved on such and such day." And if you ask them "Have you been saved?" they can point to a specific date, time and place.

We answer this question in this way. Salvation is a continuous action. It does not happen at one moment in time. Because I have been baptized and believe, I have the potential to be saved (faith). I must work towards my salvation today (works). And ultimately I will be saved by God's grace (grace). All three work in tandem.

St. Paul wrote in Ephesians 2:8–10,

> For by grace you have been saved through faith; and this
> is not your own doing, it is the gift of God—not because
> of works, lest any man should boast. For we are His work-
> manship, created in Christ Jesus for good works, which
> God prepared beforehand, that we should walk in them.

Another way to understand faith, works and grace is to take a cup, some rocks and some water. The cup represents the faith—it is the structure of what we believe. But faith without works is an empty faith. The rocks represent works. But works done without faith are like rocks spread over a table, they have no structure or goal and are ends to themselves. So we combine faith and works by putting the rocks in the cup. Yet there are still spaces in the cup that are empty. This is where the water (grace) comes in. Pour water over the rocks and the cup is filled, there are no more empty spaces.

So we combine a cup, rocks and water and we end up with a full cup. And combine faith, works and grace, and you end up with salvation. It doesn't happen in a defined moment. It happens over time. It is a daily choice. It is a daily struggle to maintain the faith and the works and keep asking for the grace.

As for the question "are you saved?" I answer with this: I have the potential to be saved. I am working on my salvation today. I hope to ultimately be saved by God's grace.

Why do I need salvation? Because I am a sinner, and as St. Paul writes in Romans 6:23, "For the wages of sin is death, but the free gift of God is eternal life in Christ Jesus our Lord." Christ coming to earth at the Nativity and dying on the Cross for my sins on Good Friday, and being Resurrected from the dead on Pascha, these are the things that open the possibility of my being saved from death. I am still going to die one day, but because of Christ my Savior, I have the potential to pass from death to life. I have the opportunity to not live in a state of eternal death, but in a state of eternal life.

> Let Your mercies quickly overtake us, for we have become very poor. Help us, O God our savior; because of the glory of Your name, O Lord, save us, and be merciful to our sins because of Your name. (Prayer from the Royal Hours. Trans. Fr. Seraphim Dedes)

Work on your salvation today!

December 1

What's In a Name?

"For to you is born this day in the city of David,
*a Savior who is **Christ the Lord**"*
—Luke 2:11

One of the things that confuses about God are the various names we call Him—or is it "Them"? The correct answer to this question is we worship ONE God, in three persons. We refer to God in the singular—Him. We pray to the Trinity—Father, Son, and Holy Spirit. Each has a specific role and each is referred to by different names. Today's reflection examines the names of God the Son.

Jesus—The earthly name given to God's Son. "She will bear a Son and you shall call His name **Jesus.** (Matt. 1:23)."

Emmanuel—"Behold a Virgin shall conceive and bear a Son, and His name shall be called **Emmanuel,** which means God with us." (Matthew 1:25)

Messiah—The promised deliverer for the people of Israel: "The woman said to Him, 'I know that **Messiah** is coming (He who is called Christ); when He comes, He will show us all things.'" (John 4:25)

The Christ—The title of the promised Messiah: "Then He strictly charged the disciples to tell no one that He was **the Christ**." (Matthew 16:20)

Lord—"And Peter said to Jesus, '**Lord**, it is well that we are here; if You wish, I will make three booths here, one for You, and one for Moses and one for Elijah.'" (Matthew 17:4, at the Transfiguration)

Savior—From the account of the Samaritan Woman: "It is no longer because of your words that we believe, for we have heard for ourselves, and we know that this is indeed the **Savior** of the world." (John 4:42)

God—"And Jesus said to Thomas, 'Put your finger here, and see My hands; and put out your hand, and place it in My side; do not be faithless, but believing.' Thomas answered Him, 'My Lord and my **God**!'" (John 20:27–28)

Master—Jesus said "neither be called masters, for you have one **Master**, the Christ." (Matthew 23:10)

The Word (in Greek, the Logos)—In the Beginning was **the Word**, and the Word was with God, and the Word was God. He was in the beginning with God; all things were made through Him, and without Him was not anything made that was made." (John 1:1–3) This, incidentally, is the theme of our whole study—"And the Word become flesh." More on this to follow.

Son of God—"And when they got into the boat, the wind ceased. And those in the boat worshipped Him, saying, 'Truly You are the **Son of God**.'" (Matthew 14:32–33)

Son of Man—"'But that you may know that the **Son of Man** has authority on earth to forgive sins'—He then said to the Paralytic—'Rise, take up your bed and go home.'" (Matthew 9:6) I have always struggled to understand what this particular title means. One meaning is that the "son of a man is a man," pointing to the humanity of Jesus. The other definition comes from the Old Testament Prophecy of Daniel and points to His divinity: "I saw in the night visions, 'and behold, with the clouds of heaven there came one like a **Son of Man**, and He came to the Ancient of Days (God) and was presented before Him. And to Him was given dominion and glory and kingdom, that all peoples, nations and languages should serve Him; His dominion is an everlasting dominion, which shall not pass away, and His kingdom one that shall not be destroyed.'" (Daniel 7: 13–14)

Son of David—Used because Jesus was a descendant of David through Joseph: "And behold, a Canaanite woman from that region came out and cried, 'Have mercy on me, O Lord, **Son of David;** my daughter is severely possessed by a demon.'" (Matthew 15:22)

Lamb of God—This title relates to the feast of the Passover, when a lamb without blemish was killed, and its blood spread over the doorposts of the houses of the Israelites in Egypt, so that when the angel of death (the tenth plague) "passed over" Egypt, it would save the children of the Israelites while the first born sons of Egypt would die (Exodus 12). Jesus is also revealed as the Lamb of God, who does the same thing for us. He died for our sins, and through His Blood we too "pass over" from death to eternal life: "The next day he (John the Baptist) saw Jesus coming toward him, and said 'Behold, **the Lamb of God**, who takes away the sin of the world!'" (John 1:29)

Light of the World—"Again Jesus spoke to them saying, 'I am the **Light of the World**; he who follows Me will not walk in darkness, but will have the Light of life.'" (John 8:12)

King of the Jews—As the Messiah was foretold to be the deliverer of the Jewish people, Jesus was also called "King of the Jews" by the Magi at His Nativity: "Where is He who has been born **King of the Jews?** For we have seen His star in the East and have come to worship Him." (Matthew 2:2) The same title was also at the Crucifixion, by those who put Him to death: "And over His head they put the charge against him, which read 'This is Jesus the **King of the Jews.**'" (Matthew 27:37)

Rabbi (which means "Teacher," another name used for Jesus)—"Nathanael answered Him, '**Rabbi**, You are the Son of God! You are the King of Israel!'" (John 1:49)

This is by no means an exhaustive list of the names given to Jesus in the Bible, but as the message to the shepherds from the angel offered the names of "Savior," "Christ," and "the Lord," I thought it would be helpful to introduce the other names given to Him as well.

Isaiah, who was one of the prophets who foretold of the coming of Christ, also offered many names for Him, in a prophecy that is read at the Royal Hours of the Nativity, as well as at the Vespers:

> For to us a child is born, to us a Son is given; and the government will be upon His shoulder, and His name will be called "Wonderful Counselor, Mighty God, Everlasting Father, Prince of Peace." Of the increase of His government and of peace there will be no end, upon the throne

of David, and over his kingdom, to establish it, and to uphold it with justice and with righteousness from this time forth and for evermore. The zeal of the Lord of hosts will do this. (Isa. 9:6–7, read at the Royal Hours of the Nativity and at the Vespers of the Nativity)

Have a great day!

December 2

God's Signs In Our Lives

And this will be a sign for you. You will find a babe wrapped
in swaddling cloths and lying in a manger.
—Luke 2:12

One of my favorite hobbies is mowing my lawn. I find it very relaxing. One of the things I have never been able to do is mow only part of the yard, leaving the rest for another day. If I'm going to mow the lawn, I do the entire thing, always! One day in summer in Florida, I was mowing the lawn, when dark clouds quickly moved in, as they are prone to do here. Dark clouds in summer is usually a sign for rain. I kept on mowing the lawn, ignoring the sign of impending rain. Sure enough, soon it began to rain. I kept on mowing, undeterred by the rain. Then it began to pour heavy rain. I was stubbornly determined to continue mowing in the downpour. In the distance, I heard the rumbling of thunder. I still wasn't deterred. I kept on mowing.

Soon the thunder got louder. Then I started thinking, maybe this wasn't the safest thing I was doing, mowing out in a thunderstorm, but the thinking still wasn't enough for me to stop. Yes, I was ignoring all the signs that I should stop—the clouds, the rain, the heavy rain, the rolling thunder, the loud thunder. Then, in the nearby vicinity, there was the bolt of lightning. And THEN I thought to myself, "This is totally crazy that I am out here mowing the lawn. It is really worth me getting hit by lightning and dying so that the lawn can all be mowed today?" So, for the one (and so far only) time in my life, I went in without finishing the job. Two days later, I went out and mowed the whole lawn over again. No, I wasn't only going to mow the part I didn't—I mowed the whole thing again.

Years later, it doesn't even matter that I didn't finish the yard that day. I ended up a little frustrated for ONE day, I got some extra exercise in and now I have a good story to tell people. Had I stayed outside, got hit by lightning and died, my child would be without a father, my wife without a husband, my parish without a priest, and my life would have been really wasted. All of that could have happened because I was stubborn and ignored the signs that I should stop mowing that summer day.

God gives signs in our lives. He gives us signs for how to behave, how to forgive, He gives us talents that we are supposed to use for His glory. Yet, how many times do we ignore these obvious signs! Is it because of our own stubbornness? Pride?

When the angel told the shepherds the good news of the Nativity of Christ, he gave the shepherds an OBVIOUS sign—that they would find a babe wrapped in swaddling clothes and lying in a manger. There was nothing tricky or confusing about this. When the shepherds came upon the Baby Jesus, there would be no doubt that they would have found what the angel was speaking about.

God gives obvious signs in our lives. We are sometimes too stubborn or too proud to heed them. We are sometimes too busy to hear them. This is where we go back to listening to God through scripture, but also watching for signs that are obvious for what God expects us to do.

I'm reminded of the joke about the person whose house was flooding and they prayed to God for deliverance and then a rowboat passed the house and the person in the boat beckoned the homeowner to row to safety. The homeowner stayed put and as the floodwaters rose, they asked

God for deliverance. A motorboat passed by and the driver beckoned the homeowner to come into the boat. But the homeowner stayed put. As the floodwaters continued to rise, the homeowner stood on the roof of the house beckoning for deliverance. A helicopter flew by and the pilot beckoned the homeowner to climb aboard. The homeowner stayed put. Eventually the homeowner was swept away by the floodwaters, and as he was about to drown, he screamed out to the Lord, "I asked you to deliver me. Why didn't you save me?" To which the Lord replied, "I sent you a rowboat, a motorboat, and a helicopter. What more did you want?"

The moral of this story is that God oftentimes is sending us signs, and we somehow manage to ignore them. There are many middle-aged people who are not happy in their work, who will admit that years ago, they felt called to do something but didn't do it because it wasn't lucrative enough. They missed a sign. Many people who are not married will admit that there was an obvious person they should have married looking back, but they missed signs as well. Many people miss signs that they need to forgive someone. Some people miss signs that they are overcommitting or overloading. We ignore signs that our health is worsening. We avoid signs that we should get help for a problem. I can't tell you how many times, for example, a couple comes in for help for their marriage that is crumbling and lament, "there were signs that we were in trouble a long time ago, and we didn't get help and now it might be too late." That's not just with marriage or health. There are many instances in life where we ignore signs that we need some help.

God provides signs, some obvious, and many subtle, which can lead us to a better understanding of His will for our lives and can lead to better lives overall for us. The question is, are we watching for them? The smart person isn't the one who stubbornly plows ahead, but the one who makes the sometimes smarter decision to stop, or to ask for help.

One lesson I have learned from speaking with my Spiritual Father, is that when I am in doubt of what God's will is for my life; if I'm not sure if a sign is from God or from my own ego, I ask God for two things: First, for His will, not mine, to be done. And secondly, for Him to make His will OBVIOUS to me, to not leave me the opportunity for second guessing. When there is an opportunity I'm not sure if I should take or not, I ask God to either roll out the red carpet for me or slam the door on me, but not to leave room for me to think about it too much.

Today's hymn is from the Royal Hours of the Nativity and it recounts for us the many signs of Christ's divinity that were present at His Nativity.

> Today He who holds the whole world in His hand is born from a Virgin.
> He who in essence is impalpable is swaddled in rags as a mortal.
> God who established the heavens of old in the beginning is lying in a manger.
> He who rained down manna for the people in the wilderness is breastfed with milk.
> He who is the Bridegroom of the Church is summoning Magi.
> And He, that Son of the Virgin, is accepting their gifts.
> We adore Your Nativity, O Christ.
> Show us also Your Divine Epiphany.
> (Hymn from the Royal Hours of the Nativity. Trans. Fr. Seraphim Dedes)

May you see all of God's signs today!

December 3

He Came with Great Humility

And this will be a sign for you. **You will find a babe wrapped
in swaddling cloths and lying in a manger.**
—Luke 2:12

For centuries, God's people had been hearing prophecies about
a promised Messiah, a deliverer. The prophecies contained
Messianic signs, things that would happen that would be the work of the
Messiah, the Christ. Isaiah wrote concerning how the people would know
who the Messiah was, that there He would reveal be several unmistakable
signs: "Then the eyes of the blind shall be opened, and the ears of the deaf
unstopped; then shall the lame man leap like a hart, and the tongue of the
dumb sing for joy (Isa. 35:5)."

But when would this happen? And how?

We know that at the time of the Nativity, the Jews (God's chosen
people) were living under the oppression of the Romans. In fact, the
census being conducted in Bethlehem was a census required by the
Romans. There is no doubt that the Roman rule was a brutal one. Civil
rights and property rights were wantonly violated. When the Jews went
to the temple and heard prophecies about their deliverance by a Messiah,
they very likely were thinking that this deliverance would be political
and military in nature. They thought their deliverer would come with
great power. A man of humility was probably the farthest thing from

their minds. They were probably expecting a powerful military general with thousands of chariots under his command. Perhaps that's why the crowds who screamed "Hosanna" for Jesus on Palm Sunday were so easily swayed to scream "crucify Him" only five days later. They were frustrated and angered that their "king" had come to Jerusalem and had not overthrown the Romans, that He had rode in alone on a donkey rather than leading an army of soldiers.

Christ came with great humility. His birth wasn't announced to the whole world. It was announced to the humble—the simple shepherds in the countryside. Even the mighty Magi, whom we will encounter shortly, showed great humility to leave their lands and follow a star for two years. As we will learn, God didn't call only the lowly, but the powerful. He calls everyone, the lowly and the powerful, to come to Him with humility.

Remember the first thing one has to believe in order to be a Christian? It is that God, who is greater than us, made us. (The second thing is that we fell from grace and the third thing is that our salvation and redemption is made possible through the death and Resurrection of Jesus Christ, which is set in motion through His Incarnation). And if we believe that God made us, One who is greater than us made us, then we are not the center of the universe, our universe or any other universe.

When we think *it's all about me*, that is arrogance. When we think *It's not about me*, that is humility. When we think *it's about my neighbor,* that is humility. When we think *it's about Him (God)*, that is humility.

Christ shows us not only the way back to Paradise. He shows us the way to humility. His birth is simple, not grand. He is born in a cave, not the best inn in Bethlehem. His is adored by simple shepherds, not by the populace gathered in Bethlehem for the census. He is wrapped in swaddling clothes, not the fine linens of a king. He is laid in a manger, not set on a throne; and He tells us that His Kingdom is based on humility, not on might.

In Matthew 5, Jesus offers us the Beatitudes, the guideposts for living a life in God. All are based on humility:

> Blessed are the poor in spirit, for theirs is the kingdom of heaven.
> Blessed are those who mourn, for they shall be comforted.
> Blessed are the meek, for they shall inherit the earth.
> Blessed are those who hunger and thirst for righteousness, for they shall be satisfied.
> Blessed are the merciful, for they shall obtain mercy.
> Blessed are the pure in heart, for they shall see God.
> Blessed are the peacemakers, for they shall be called sons of God.
> Blessed are those who are persecuted for righteousness' sake, for theirs is the kingdom of heaven.
> Blessed are you when men revile you and persecute you and utter all kinds of evil against you falsely on My account. Rejoice and be glad, for your reward is great in heaven. (Matt. 5:3–12)

We seem to demand so much in our lives. Many times, it becomes all about me, and not about Him. In many ways, Christmas has become a feast of material gain, as our children make lists of what they want for Christmas. The Nativity is a feast of SPIRITUAL gain. And we only gain spiritually through humility—when we bend a knee in prayer, when we come to God in repentance, when we serve our neighbor. Honoring God in your life doesn't necessarily bring fame or fortune. It brings something even more important—treasure in heaven. Jesus tells us:

> Do not lay up for yourselves treasures on earth, where moth and rust consume and where thieves break in and steal, but lay up for yourselves treasures in heaven, where neither moth nor rust consumes and where thieves to not break in and steal. For where your treasure is, there will your heart be also. (Matt. 6:19–20)

As we prepare for the Nativity, teach your children and remember for yourself, that the treasure of the feast is not what lies under the Christmas tree ready to be torn open on Christmas morning. The greatest treasure of the feast is Christ Himself. And He is opened not only on Christmas morning, but can be opened at any time—through prayer, through faith, through service. And the root of all of these things is humility.

It's not about me. It's all about HIM!

> He is our God: There is no other to compare with Him. Born of a Virgin, He comes to live with mankind. The only-begotten Son appears as a mortal Man. He rests in a lowly manger. The Lord of Glory is wrapped in swaddling clothes. A star leads the wise men to worship Him, and with them we sing: Holy Trinity, save our souls! (Hymn from the Royal Hours of the Nativity. Trans. Fr. Seraphim Dedes)

Live for Him today!

December 4

Who Are the Angels?

And suddenly there was with the angel a multitude
of the heavenly host, praising God.
Luke 2:13

Who are the angels? They figure very prominently in the Nativity story. And they are mentioned sporadically throughout the Bible.

In Genesis 3, after the Fall of mankind, we read that God "drove out the man (from the Garden of Eden); and at the east of the Garden of Eden He placed the Cherubim, and a flaming sword which turned every way, to guard the way to the Tree of Life (Gen. 3:24)." Orthodox tradition holds that this is the Archangel Michael. This is why on the icon screen of every church, the Archangel Michael is depicted on the left side of the icon screen. His icon is a door from which all processions begin. The procession "comes out" of the Archangel Michael door, because he guards the door from which we "came out" of the Garden of Eden.

In Isaiah 6, the Prophet speaks of a vision of the Seraphim, another type of angel:

> I saw the Lord sitting upon a throne, high and lifted up; and His train filled the temple. Above Him stood the Seraphim; each had six wings: with two he covered his

face, and with two he covered his feet, and with two he flew. And one called to another and said: "Holy, holy, holy is the Lord of Hosts; the whole earth is full of His glory." (Isa. 6:1–3)

The Psalms speak of a Guardian Angel, who watches over us:

Because you have made the Lord your refuge, the Most High your habitation, no evil shall befall you, no scourge come near your tent. For He will give His angels charge of you to guard you in all your ways. On their hands, they will bear you up. (Ps. 91:9–12)

Cartoons often depict a white angel sitting on the shoulder of a character, encouraging him or her to make a good decision, with a red devil sitting on the other shoulder, tempting him or her to make a bad one. And while we do not depict such a thing in our iconography, we believe both that the devil comes to tempt us (not necessarily in obvious ways like a red-horned man sitting on our shoulder but through more subtle ways) and that angels come to guard, guide and protect us. Though we do not have a white angel sitting on our shoulders, we believe that we have guardian angels, unseen guardians that guide and guard us.

The angels bring messages from God to us. The Archangel Gabriel figures prominently in the Nativity narrative. In Luke 1:19, it is the Archangel Gabriel who tells Zacharias that he and Elizabeth would bear the Forerunner of Christ in their old age: "And the angel answered him, 'I am Gabriel, who stands in the presence of God; and I was sent to speak to you, and to bring you this good news.' (Luke 1:19)" It is also the Archangel Gabriel who makes the Annunciation to the Virgin Mary: "In the sixth month the angel Gabriel was sent from God to a city of Galilee named Nazareth, to a Virgin betrothed to a men whose name was Joseph, of the house of David; and the Virgin's name was Mary. And he came to her and said: 'Hail, O Favored One, the Lord is with you!' (Luke 1:26–28)"

The angels were created by God. Orthodox theology holds that there are nine orders of angels: Angels, Archangels, Thrones, Dominions, Principalities, Authorities, Powers, the Cherubim and the Seraphim. In Colossians 1:15–16, St. Paul writes:

> He (Christ) is the image of the invisible God, the first-born of all creation; for in Him all things were created, in heaven and on earth, visible and invisible, whether thrones or dominions or principalities or authorities— all things were created through Him and for Him." And St. Basil, in the Anaphora of his liturgy, writes: For You are praised by the angels, archangels, thrones, dominions, principalities, authorities, powers and the many eyed Cherubim. Round about you stand the Seraphim, one with six wings, and the other with six wings; with two they cover their faces; with two they cover their feet; with two they fly, crying out to one another with unceasing voices and ever-resounding praises. (Liturgy of St. Basil. Trans. Holy Cross Seminary Press)

So, the role of the angels are to be God's messengers. In the Nativity account, the Archangel delivered the news to the Virgin Mary of the Incarnation of Christ. And the multitude of the heavenly host delivered the message to the Shepherds. How AWESOME it must have been for even one angel to deliver the good news. But then imagine a multitude of the heavenly hosts appeared, surrounded by God's glory, what a sight that must have been to behold. It would be beyond awesome. And STILL the busy city of Bethlehem did not notice—that almost seems to defy comprehension as well.

We, too, are surrounded by angels that guide us, guard us and give us messages and signs from God. Are we like the shepherds, in awe of the message? Or are we like Bethlehem, totally oblivious?

One more comment on angels, which is this—God sent His angels to guard, guide, and protect us. However, He has also empowered US to play this role for one another. If God can work through powers that are unseen, He most certainly can work through people who ARE seen. We also must take on the role of angels, in the sense of encouraging people to do what is good, and encouraging others to do what pleases God. If we hope to one day be with the angels, then we must learn to act like angels as well.

> Praise Him, all you His angels; praise Him, all you His hosts. To You, O God is due our song.
> (The Praises, Orthros of the Nativity. Trans. Fr. Seraphim Dedes)

Be *angelic* today!

December 5

Praising God

And suddenly there was with the angel a multitude
*of the heavenly host, **praising God**.*
—Luke 2:13

There are four elements that should comprise a prayer: Praise, Thanksgiving, Confession, and Supplication. Most of us are familiar with the supplication part. Many prayers include supplication only. Unfortunately, many people pray only when they want to ask God for something. Prayer should include confession and repentance; an examination of what we've done wrong on a particular day; and how we can do it better next time. Prayer should include thanksgiving to God for what He does for us.

Prayer, however, should begin with praise and worship of God. Merely invoking the name of God is worship. "Dear God," "Heavenly Father," "O Christ our Savior," "Almighty Lord," "Our Father" are all ways that we are familiar with opening prayer. "Lord, have mercy" is one of the shortest prayers. But even this prayer, which asks for mercy, begins with a statement of worship, "LORD, have mercy."

To praise God acknowledges that God is greater than us. We come to God not in self-righteousness, but in humility.

In Luke 18: 10–14, Jesus tells us the Parable of the Publican and the Pharisee:

Two men went up into the temple to pray, one a Pharisee and the other a tax collector. The Pharisee stood and prayed thus with himself, "God, I thank Thee that I am not like other men, extortioners, unjust, adulterers, or even like this tax collector. I fast twice a week, I give tithes of all that I get." But the tax collector, standing far off, would not even lift his eyes to heaven, but beat his breast, saying "God, be merciful to me a sinner!" I tell you, this man went down to his house justified rather than the other; for everyone who exalts himself will be humbled, but he who humbles himself will be exalted.

The prayer of a righteous man does not boast of what one has done, but what he has yet to do. And praise of God is not about congratulating ourselves about how far we have come, but acknowledging humbly before God how far we have to go, and asking for His help in getting there. Worship and praise of God are done to help us get closer to God. Worship and praise can only be effective if we acknowledge that we have a ways to go to get to God.

The postures we take in worship help us understand what "praise of God" is. We stand in order to present ourselves at attention. This is why there isn't a lot of sitting in church, because when we sit, we relax and are casual. When we stand, we are at attention. When Christ healed the Paralytic, He commanded him to "rise, take up your pallet and go home. (Mark 2:11)." Even though we are sinful, when we receive Communion, we stand at attention, presenting ourselves fully to God for the spiritual healing that comes through receiving Him in Communion.

Bowing is part of our worship experience. We bow our heads to pray. When we are called to worship at the Small Entrance, we sing, "Come let us worship and bow down before Christ."

And we kneel in awe of God. As we call the Holy Spirit "upon us and upon these Gifts here presented," we get on our knees in awe of God's presence among us through the descent of the Holy Spirit in our midst.

If Christianity is about loving God and loving our neighbor, then the posture we take in prayer when we praise God should also be the posture we take as we serve our neighbor. When our neighbor is speaking, we should be at attention, listening attentively. When we serve our neighbor, we should "bow" in humility. It's not always about us winning or succeeding. Serving our neighbor is about putting our neighbor in front of us and our needs. And we should hold our neighbor in respect, if not awe, since our neighbor is made in God's image and likeness, just like we are.

I will end today's reflection by telling the story about a man named "Jim" (not his real name). I didn't know Jim for most of his life, as Jim had not been a faithful Christian for most of his life. Jim was diagnosed with cancer at a relatively young age. He only lived about six months between his diagnosis and death. During those six months, as he waged a losing battle with his disease, by God's grace I helped him wage a winning battle for his soul. This man who never went to church, was in church every Sunday. This man who had never read the Bible, read it cover to cover. This man, who had hardly ever spoken to a priest, was talking to me almost every week. When I heard his last confession a few days before he died, as he lay in bed very much in pain, he asked me if I would help him get on his knees so I could offer the prayer of absolution over him while he was kneeling. When I told him that that wasn't really necessary, that I could offer the prayer with him lying in bed, he looked at me, and with tears in his eyes, said to me "Please, Father, help me to get on my knees. I want to kneel in front of God one more time before I go to Him for the judgment of my soul." It took four of us to lift him out of bed, gently place him on his knees on the floor, and then to put him back in bed. I will never forget the sincerity of his last prayer and the humility of this last request, a witness of faith that still inspires me to this day.

The angels who shared the good news with the shepherds, who praised God in the skies over Bethlehem, were not making a show of themselves. They were joyfully witnessing for God. Let us be inspired to do the same. It is not possible for every word we say to "praise God." But it is possible in every, and any, breath, to give God praise.

> Let every breath praise the Lord. Praise the Lord from the heavens, praise Him in the highest. To You, O God is due our song. (The Praises, Orthros of the Nativity. Trans. Fr. Seraphim Dedes)

Praise God today!

December 6

What is Peace?

*And suddenly there was with the angel a multitude of the heavenly host, praising God, and saying, "Glory to God in the highest, **and on earth peace** among men with whom He is pleased!"*
—Luke 2:13–14

What is peace? I'm sure if you polled people in various countries, you'd get a different answer. To the person in the war-torn Middle East, peace is the absence of gunfire. To the monk on Mount Athos, peace is the absence of spiritual conflict. The common denominator in any definition of peace is that it involves an absence of some kind of conflict.

At the time of Christ's Nativity, there were many conflicts in Bethlehem and surrounding regions. The most obvious conflict was between the Jews and their Romans oppressors. It was a military/political/economic conflict. The Romans held an overpowering position in all of these areas. There was a religious conflict between Jews and Gentiles. The Jews identified themselves as "God's chosen people," and were not friendly with Gentiles (non-Jews). Many times in the Bible we read about conflicts between the Jews and Samaritans. There was even conflict among the Jews. A class of elite temple leadership preyed on the Jewish populace, binding heavy burdens on their own people. Even the journey to Bethlehem for the census could not have been a peaceful one. Lots of traffic, lots of people converging on a small town, fighting for rooms at inns (remember they were all filled), food most likely in short supply, and tempers probably flaring as well. The peace of the cave where the Nativity took place and the stillness of the countryside where it was announced to the shepherds were quite a contrast to the upheaval all around. It's no wonder that the "Prince of Peace," our Lord, came to us in the peaceful setting where He was born.

Many "protests" have been waged in the name of "world peace." The running joke in beauty pageant scenes in movies is the answer that every contestant gives to the question of what one thing would you like to change in the world: world peace.

Before we can have peace on a macro level (the world), we must learn to find peace on a micro level (within ourselves and with those around us). Before we can talk about peace in the world, we must find peace within ourselves. We must seek to rid ourselves of conflict. We must bring peace into our marriages, into the lives of our children, into the lives of our neighbors that we see every day.

If peace is the absence of conflict, then we must strive to remove conflict from ourselves and from our relationships. How is this done? It is done with patience that allows us to overlook things that take away our peace. It is done with respect that allows us to speak the truth in love when confronting someone or something that is taking our peace. It is done with honesty, that we can have a conversation with others about the things that threaten our peace and work toward a mutual goal of restoring peace.

Peace in the world begins with peace with yourself. It takes a next step when we seek to be peacemakers and not peace-takers. It is when we learn to come into a situation bringing peace and seeking peace, rather than bringing chaos and always seeking victory.

Mother Teresa describes how to find peace in this beautiful quote:

The fruit of silence is prayer.
The fruit of prayer is faith.
The fruit of faith is love.
The fruit of love is service.
The fruit of service is peace.

Indeed, prayer points us to faith, which points us to love, which points us to service. And service is where we bring peace to someone else by serving someone other than ourselves. Thus, peace is found in service to others. When I am serving, I am taking something from me and GIVING it freely to someone else. This promotes peace. When I am taking something from someone and making it mind, this is what disturbs and distorts peace and creates conflict.

In our Orthodox Liturgical services, we are called continually to peace:

"In peace let us pray to the Lord."
"For the peace from Above and the salvation of our souls,
    let us pray to the Lord."
"For peace in the whole world, the stability of the holy
    churches of God and for the unity of all, let us prayer to
    the Lord."

Before the Gospel (God's word), before the Creed (the confession of our Faith) and before Holy Communion, the priest says "peace be with you all." He says this to remind us that through Christ we can find peace, and that we find Christ by serving one another. In fact, we can only come towards Christ if we have a peaceful disposition. We do not need intellect or fortune, but we do need peace.

Today's hymn comes from the Orthros of the Nativity. If, as the hymn says, we are to "glorify in a manner fitting God the babe that is born," then we must learn the meaning of peace and all the things that precede it—prayer, faith, love and service. Christ embodied all of these things. Let us seek to be like Him by doing the same.

> Glory to God in the highest, and peace on earth. Today Bethlehem receives Him who is ever seated with the Father. Today Angels glorify in a manner fitting God the babe that is born. Glory to God in the highest, and on earth peace, and good will among men. (Idiomelon from the Orthros of the Nativity. Trans. Fr. Seraphim Dedes)

Be a peacemaker today!

December 7

What? Peace Is Not for Everyone?

*"Glory to God in the highest, and on earth **peace among men
with whom He is pleased!**"*
—*Luke 2:14*

Most of us are familiar with the hymn of the Angels at the Nativity. Most often we remember it as "Glory to God in the highest, and on earth peace, goodwill towards men." This translation denotes that God's gift of peace is for all people. Certainly, His **wish** is for peace to reign among all people. But the most correct translation of this phrase is "Glory to God in the highest, and on earth, peace *among men with whom He is pleased!*" In this translation, we learn that peace is not a right granted to everyone who merely lives and breathes, but rather it is a Gift, a Fruit of the Spirit (Gal. 5:22) that is bestowed upon those who please God. Peace is a trait that is cultivated by each person, and those who cultivate it well, reap the fruit of their work.

The easiest way to understand the hymn of the angels is this: Peace is available to anyone who wishes to work for it. Now, what kind of peace are we talking about here? Because one can work as hard as they want and still may not be able to escape the violence of a war-torn country or rough neighborhood.

St. Paul writes in his Epistle to the Philippians:

Have no anxiety about anything, but in everything by prayer and supplication with thanksgiving let your requests be made known to God. And the peace of God, which passes all understanding, will keep your hearts and minds in Christ Jesus. (Phil. 4:6–7)

There is a spiritual peace that can only come from God. This peace passes all understanding, because it is neither a military peace nor a material peace. For those who know the peace of God, they have this intangible quality about them. They almost seem to rise above petty conflict. This kind of peace is cultivated through prayer and meditation on the scriptures. It is also found in service to others.

As a practical matter then, if you want peace, focus on being grateful first and foremost. Being jealous about what you don't have often leads to conflict. Being grateful for what you do have is a step towards peace. Focusing on God through prayer brings peace. Losing sight of God brings conflict, so make dedicated time each day to focus on God. And as we do in the liturgical services, make offering a prayer for personal peace as well as peace in the world part of your daily prayer ritual.

One of my favorite songs that is played during the Christmas season is "Let There Be Peace on Earth and Let It Begin with Me" by Sy Miller and Jill Jackson. The lyrics are as follows:

Let there be peace on earth and let it begin with me.
Let there be peace on earth the peace that was meant to be.
With God as our Father, brothers all are we.
Let me walk with my brother, in perfect harmony.

Let peace begin with me let this be the moment now.

With every step I take let this be my solemn vow.

To take each moment and live each moment in peace eternally.

Let there be peace on earth and let it begin with me.

I remember a few years back, there was a school shooting at an elementary school in Newtown, Connecticut. Twenty-six students and teachers were killed. This happened only two days before our Sunday school Christmas program was scheduled. I remember thinking was it even appropriate for our children to be singing and laughing when in Connecticut, there was mourning for children the same age as our children doing the program. We decided that we would have the program but that we would conclude it with this song. And when the time came, I remember asking for all of the doors to the church to be opened, so that symbolically we could sing this song to the whole world. Indeed, if we are to bring peace into the world, it starts with us, with our individual witness for God, in peace and in service to others. If we truly want peace, we must first do what is pleasing to God by making Him the source and center of our lives. Then we can find peace as individuals, and then in small groups and then in large groups and then build from there.

Today's hymn is called the "Great Doxology," which precedes the Divine Liturgy just about every time the Liturgy is celebrated. It is actually the last hymn of the Orthros, or Matins, service. It incorporates all the elements of prayer—glory (Glory be to You who showed us the Light), thanksgiving (We praise You, we bless You, we worship You, we glorify You, we give thanks to You), repentance (Heal my soul, for I have sinned against You), and supplication (teach me to do Your will, for You are my God . . . have mercy on us). But the Doxology begins with the Hymn of the Angels, chanted for the shepherds as they announced the Incarnation of the Son of God in the flesh. The Doxology not only gives glory to God as we begin a new day on the calendar, but it continually reminds us of the "New Day" that dawned in the history of humanity, when the Creator became part of His creation at the feast of the Nativity. Remember, it's Christmas all year round in our church!

> Glory be to You who showed the Light. Glory in the highest to God. His peace is on earth, His good pleasure in mankind.
>
> We praise You, we bless You, we worship You, we glorify You, we give thanks to You for Your great glory.
>
> Lord King, heavenly God, Father, Ruler over all; Lord, only-begotten Son, Jesus Christ, and You, O Holy Spirit.
>
> Lord God, Lamb of God, Son of the Father, who take away the sin of the world, have mercy on us, You who take away the sins of the world.
>
> Accept our supplication, You who sit at the right hand of the Father, and have mercy on us.
>
> For You alone are holy, You alone are Lord, Jesus Christ, to the glory of God the Father. Amen.
>
> Every day I will bless You, and Your name will I praise to eternity, and to the ages of ages.
>
> Vouchsafe, O Lord, this day, that we be kept without sin.
>
> Blessed are You, O Lord, the God of our fathers, and praised and glorified is Your name to the ages. Amen.
>
> Let Your mercy be on us, O Lord, as we have set our hope on You.
>
> Blessed are You, O Lord, Teach me Your statutes.

Lord, You have been our refuge from generation to generation. I said: Lord have mercy on me. Heal my soul, for I have sinned against You.

Lord, I have fled to You. Teach me to do Your will, for You are my God.

For with You is the fountain of life; in Your light we shall see light.

Continue Your mercy to those who know You.

Holy God, Holy Mighty, Holy Immortal, have mercy on us (3)

(Great Doxology. Trans. Fr. Seraphim Dedes)

Have a peaceful day!

December 8

Be a Doer!

When the angels went away from them into heaven, the shepherds said to one another, **"Let us go** *over to Bethlehem and see this thing that has happened, which the Lord has made known to us."*
—Luke 2:15

Can you imagine if, after the message of the angel, seeing the glory of God and hearing the heavenly choir of angels sing, the shepherds said "well, that was nice, but back to business as usual," and just kept sitting in the field?

It's actually easy to imagine if you think about it, because this is exactly what many people do. They attend services on Christmas (and some not even that), have dinner, open gifts, and eventually eat the leftovers, put away the decorations, and life goes on as before.

In the Orthodox world, we have a greeting we are supposed to give at the Feast of the Nativity. We say "Christ is Born!" And the response is "Glorify Him!" This is not only a saying but a directive. Christ is born, now go to action. The Nativity was the catalyst for Christ's earthly ministry. It is supposed to be a catalyst to us as well.

Perhaps the key moment in the life of a Christian is that moment they go from *hearer* to *doer*. Many of us have heard the message from our infancy. We come into church as babies and young children. We *hear* but what do we really *understand*? Unfortunately, for many, their faith is like that of a young child—they hear and that's about where it stops.

The next step in the journey is *understanding*. This comes when we hear with a mind and a heart that are open to receiving a message, not just hearing a message. This step also involves study. We have to open the Bible, read a theology book, perhaps take an Orthodoxy 101 class, so that we can understand what it is we are hearing.

But the ultimate and necessary step is when understanding translates into action, when we move from *hearers* to *doers*. From our infancy, we are told to pray. In our youth and young adult life, hopefully we learn how to pray. Then we begin to pray, and start becoming one who prays regularly (a doer) and then we learn not only what it means to pray but the power of prayer.

Same thing goes for loving our neighbor. At pre-school, we learned "hands are for helping, not for hitting." In our teen years (and hopefully even sooner), we are exposed to service projects to help us learn the meaning of service and that there are people who are in need of services we can provide. Hopefully as we grow and mature, in life and in faith, we make service to others more central to our lives.

Again, let's go back to the account of the Nativity. Can you imagine if the shepherds only heard but didn't go? If the Magi saw the star but decided, "that's nice, but we'll stay put in our land"? Or if Joseph had heard the angel tell him to get out of Bethlehem and flee to Egypt so Jesus wouldn't be killed by Herod, if he said "that's okay, we'll just stay here?" Noah, Abraham, Jacob, Moses, Isaiah, Peter, Paul—we've got dozens of examples in the Bible of people who heard the word of God and then did something about it. Our role is the same—putting what we have heard into action. It is not enough to hear, but to do.

On a practical level, each morning when you wake up, think of something you can do to show your love for God and something else you can do to show love for your neighbor. Make a daily plan to DO something that will glorify God and help your neighbor.

I'm reminded of the story of the boy walking on the beach covered with tens of thousands of starfish that would certainly die if out of the water. The boy picked up a starfish and threw it back into the water. Then he picked up another and another and another. An older man was walking on the beach and said to the boy, "you are throwing many starfish into the water, but there are more starfish here than you can count. What possible difference can you make?" The boy picked up a starfish and threw it into the water, looked at the older man and said "well, I made a difference for that one." (Adapted from *The Star Thrower* by Loren Eiseley)

We can't change the whole world but we can certainly make a difference in our corner of it. It's not enough to see the starfish and say, "this is a problem." And it's not really productive to look at the overwhelming number of starfish and say, "I can't save them all." The doer says to himself, "I can make a difference for that one," and then does it.

Going back to the song I mentioned in the last reflection, none of us can bring peace to the whole earth all by ourselves. But we can be seekers of peace, and doers of things that promote peace. It doesn't say, "let there be peace on earth and let it end with me." It says, "Let there be peace on earth and let it *begin* with ME." Making a difference in your relationship with God and with your neighbor begins the moment you reach the conclusion that the shepherds did, when you decide "let us go," and you move from hearer to doer.

Come, believer let us see the place where Christ has been born. With the Magi, those three kings who from the orient are, now let us follow to where the star is proceeding. Ceaselessly do Angels sing praises there. Shepherds in the field sing a worthy song, saying: Glory in the highest be to Him who was born today in the grotto from the Virgin and Theotokos, in Bethlehem of Judea. (Kathisma from the Orthros of the Nativity. Trans. Fr. Seraphim Dedes)

Go do it!

December 9

TODAY!

*And **they went with haste**, and found Mary and Joseph*
and babe lying in a manger.
—Luke 2:16

The shepherds looked at each other, mulled over what to do, and decided that not only they had to go see what the angels were talking about, but they had to go right now, with a sense of urgency. The Bible is filled with examples of people who went with haste.

When Jesus called the first disciples, Andrew and Peter, we are told that, "Immediately they left their nets and followed Him (Matt. 4:20)." When He called James and John, the sons of Zebedee, "Immediately they left the boat and their father, and followed Him (Matt. 4:22)."

When Jesus told the Paralytic to take up his pallet and walk, "he rose and immediately took up the pallet and went out before them all (Mark 2:12)." Jesus healed a blind man who instantly became a disciple: "Immediately he received his sight and followed Him, glorifying God (Luke 18:43)." There was a man who wished for his son to be healed. "Jesus said to him, 'If you can! All things are possible to him who believes.' Immediately the father of the child cried out and said 'I believe; help my unbelief!' (Mark 9:23–24)" All of these people encountered Christ, were ministered to, and immediately ran to Christ.

One of the most stunning turnarounds in the Bible is the story of Zacchaeus, a notorious tax collector who was the town pariah. Desiring to see who Jesus was, but unable to because he was short and unpopular, he ran up ahead and climbed into a sycamore tree. When Jesus saw him, He said "Zacchaeus, make haste and come down; for I must stay at your house today." So he made haste and came down and received Him joyfully (Luke 19:5–6)." Zacchaeus was a changed man because he heard the call of Christ. He repented and restored those who he had previously defrauded four times the value of what he had stolen.

So, we must follow the examples of immediacy from the shepherds, Zacchaeus, the disciples and the others. We need to make the most out of today and do it TODAY, because today is all that we have. We do not have yesterday—that is over. And we have no guarantee of tomorrow. We don't even have a guarantee of later today. The only thing we have as a guarantee is the moment we are in right now. If the Lord comes at this very moment for your soul, He will undoubtedly be pleased to find you reading something edifying about His Nativity. If God comes looking for you later today, where will He find you? What will He find you doing?

We shouldn't put off loving God or loving our neighbor because today might be the last day to do either. If your faith is not where you want it to be, if your prayer life is not where you want it to be, if your understanding of the scriptures is not where you want it to be, if your service to others is not where you want it to be, and most important, if these things are not where GOD wants and expects them to be, then go with haste and make inroads in these things. For time passes quickly. We only have a finite number of Christmases (and this number is only known by God) to understand the message of the Nativity. And we only have a finite number of years (and this number is only known by God) to put in to practice the things that we learn about God.

Don't let another day go by that you don't pray, don't read scripture, don't serve others, and don't let another day go by that you don't laugh and have joy, because "This is the day that the Lord has made (Ps. 118:24)," and not only are we to "rejoice and be glad in it" but we are to get the most out of it and we are to glorify God in it.

> Come, let us extol and praise the Savior's Mother, who remained a virgin even after childbirth. Animate City of our King and God, rejoice, for Christ having dwelt in you has wrought our salvation. Together with Gabriel we sing your praise, together with the shepherds we glorify you, crying out, "Theotokos, intercede with the Lord, who is incarnate from you, to save us." (The Praises, Orthros of the Nativity. Trans. Fr. Seraphim Dedes)

Do what pleases God TODAY!

December 10

Let's Talk About It

*And when they saw it **they made known the saying**
which had been told them concerning this child.*
—Luke 2:17

One of the most boisterous carols of the Christmas season is called "Go Tell It on the Mountain:"

> Go tell it on the mountain, over the hills and everywhere.
> Go tell it on the mountain, that Jesus Christ is born.

After the shepherds heard the message of the angel, saw the glory of God and heard the heavenly choir, they decided to go, and to go with haste to see what the angel had spoken about, the Babe in the manger. They went and found Mary and Joseph and the baby Jesus in the manger, just as the angels had said.

Imagine if the story had stopped here. Imagine if the shepherds did everything that they did, saw everything they saw, and then said nothing to anyone. Who would have known about the Nativity?

If you think about it, the sin we commit most in our lives is that we gossip. Hardly a day goes by that we don't speak in some unflattering or untruthful way about someone. We all do it. It's like we are almost addicted to it! Like we can't go even one day without it!

So if we like to spread bad news often, why is it that we don't want to spread the GOOD news even more? We are supposed to "go tell it on the mountain," in our homes, to our neighbors, to our children, with our spouses. We are supposed to make known the things of God to other people.

The shepherds made known the saying that was told to them by the angels. They didn't worry if they would be talked about, or ridiculed or scorned. They were moved by what they had seen—a message from an angel, the glory of the Lord, the hymn of the heavenly hosts, the baby in the manger, the tender love of His mother, the solid protection of Joseph.

How many times in your experience have you been part of a conversation that was completely negative? We've all had this experience. Many times I feel like saying "tell me something good."

God is not a God of negativity, but a God of peace, love and joy. St. Paul writes in his Epistle to the Galatians, that

> [T]he fruit of the Spirit is love, joy, peace, patience, kindness, goodness, faithfulness, gentleness, self-control; against such there is no law." (Galatians 5:22–23) He also warns us that "the works of the flesh are plain: fornication, impurity, licentiousness, idolatry, sorcery, enmity, strife, jealousy, anger, selfishness, dissension, party spirit, envy, drunkenness, carousing and the like. I warn you, as I warned you before, that those who do such things shall not inherit the kingdom of God. (Gal. 5:19–21)

We need more talking about God, more cultivating of the Fruits of the Spirit, and less encouragement towards the works of the flesh.

Do you ever talk about the Lord with anyone? If not, why not? I'm not talking about making a theology presentation, but merely saying to another person, "being a Christian makes a big difference in my life." This is something we need to say to others—to encourage them, for them to encourage us, to get us talking about the Good News.

If you read the Bible carefully, you will discover that there were many "evangelists," people who shared the good news, not just the four Gospel writers. The first "evangelists" were, in fact, the shepherds. A man who had been healed of demonic possession by Jesus "went away, proclaiming throughout the whole city how much Jesus had done for him (Luke 8:39)." A Samaritan woman (Samaritans were sworn enemies of the Jews) had a conversation with Jesus and "went away into the city and said to the people, 'come, see a man who told me all that I ever did. Can this be the Christ?' . . . Many Samaritans from that city believed in Him because of the woman's testimony (John 4: 28–29, 39)." And don't forget, the chosen disciples were mostly illiterate fisherman.

There are no qualifications needed to tell people about the Lord. Just faith and desire to share it. We're so eager to spread bad news. Let's show the same enthusiasm and talk about the Good News!

> Now the prophesy draws near to its fulfillment which mystically foretold "And you, O Bethlehem in the land of Judah, are not the least among the princes, preparing as you do the cave; for our of you shall come forth unto me a Governor of the Nations in the flesh born of a virgin Maiden, Christ our God who as a shepherd shall tend His people, the new Israel." Let us all give Him glory. (Hymn from the Royal Hours of the Nativity. Trans. Seraphim Dedes)

Remember the Lord in at least one conversation today!

December 11

What Will People Say?

*And **all who heard it wondered** at what the shepherds told them.*
—Luke 2:18

The shepherds heard the message, they went and witnessed the Baby Jesus with their own eyes, and then they told others what they had seen. And all who heard what the shepherds had to say wondered; they gave some thought to what they had heard.

Undoubtedly, some of the reaction might have been negative: "Who are these poor shepherds to talk to me?"

Some of the reaction might have been cynical: "Are these guys for real? Are they trying to work their way into our social circle by sharing some outlandish news?"

Some of the reaction might have been doubtful: "Who could believe such a tale—angels speaking, the glory of the Lord all over the sky, certainly I would have noticed."

And at best, the reaction was probably curiosity: "This is interesting, maybe I should venture over to the cave and see this for myself."

No one believed in Christ because of the testimony of the shepherds. Because to believe in Christ, one has to know Christ in a personal way. The shepherds TOLD people about Christ, and perhaps, some, out of curiosity, investigated. And if they did, then perhaps some of them believed for themselves. But without the testimony of the shepherds, there would have been no curiosity. After all, no one can accept an invitation if one is not offered.

Most of us are familiar with the Parable of the Sower (Luke 8:5–15). A sower went out and sowed his seed, and some fell on the path and was trodden underfoot. And some fell on rocks and was washed away by rain. Some fell on thorns which choked the seed. And some fell on good soil and yielded a hundredfold.

Jesus tells us the meaning of this parable. The seed is the Word of God. Those along the path are those who have heard. Some hear the Word but it never really penetrates their souls. Some hear it with joy but in time of temptation fall away. Some hear the Word with joy but are caught in the business of life and their seed never matures. And some hear the Word and hold it fast with a good heart.

I remember as a young priest feeling frustrated that I didn't see the fruit of my work maturing in front of my own eyes. And I remember my Spiritual Father talking to me about the parable of the sower. He said "imagine that in your life, you have a large bag of seed. You walk down the path and scatter seed wherever you go. At the end of the day, you put the bag down, rest, and the next day you keep scattering seed. However, you never get to turn around and look back at the seed you've scattered and you never get to pass that way again. You have to be content with scattering the seed, knowing you won't see it grow. Most importantly, God is not going to reward you based on how the seed grew, but on how much seed you threw. For the soil the seed lands in is the hearts of people, and you cannot control that. You *can* control how much seed you throw."

This message about the sowing of the seed is not only for priests, but for all people. We are all receivers of the seed, but we are also supposed to be sowers of the seed. Just like an apple tree produces apples, and each apple has a core that has a seed that can be planted to make a new apple tree, we are supposed to receive the seed, make sure that it grows and matures in us, and then spread our seeds so that more trees (more souls) can be grown for Christ. Christ will not ask us how many trees grew because of our seeds but how many seeds did we throw, how many trees did we help plant. Just like He is not going to ask me how many people came to Liturgy or Bible study, but how many Liturgies and Bible studies did I offer.

The shepherds did what they were supposed to do—they talked to people about the Lord. And perhaps they were ridiculed for it. Over the centuries, people have spoken about Christ and have been killed for it. But when you witness for Christ in a genuine way, it causes people to wonder. And while they are wondering, some are curious and they go and investigate and they find Christ.

The Gospel of Christ cannot go anywhere unless we spread it. The shepherds were hearers of the Word who became spreaders of the Word. You and I are called to do the same. We have heard. We must learn to spread the Gospel as well. How people react is not our concern. It's not how many seeds that we throw mature but how many seeds we throw that God is concerned with. Make sure that the soil in your heart is good soil, so the seed can grow in you. And as your fruit matures, take some seed and plant new trees.

> May God be gracious to us and bless us and make His face to shine upon us, that Thy way may be known upon earth, Thy saving power among all nations. Let the peoples praise Thee, O God; let all the peoples praise Thee! Let the nations be glad and sing for joy, for Thou dost judge the peoples with equity and guide the nations upon earth. Let the people praise Thee, O God; let all

the peoples praise Thee! The earth has yielded its increase; God, our God, has blessed us. God has blessed us; let all the ends of the earth fear Him! (Psalm 67, read at the Royal Hours of the Nativity.)

Grow in Christ today!

December 12

I Need to Think about This!

*But Mary kept all these things, **pondering them in her heart.***
Luke 2:19

 read in a book recently that saying, "I'm busy" is akin to saying, "I'm alive." Who, after all, is *not* busy these days? Many of us even say that we are "crazy busy." If you think about it though, we *all* have mental down time. Even when we are "working," we are not mentally occupied at all moments of the day. If I'm running copies at the office, I'm working with my hands, but not necessarily with my mind. If I honestly audit my time, I actually find I have a lot of time that I'm not mentally engaged. What fills the time when you are driving? Noise on the radio? What fills your mind while you are getting dressed, or combing your hair, or brushing your teeth, cooking, mowing, vacuuming? You get the idea.

In the mental free time that we all have, how much, if any, is spent pondering the things of God? We've all spent time pondering what we would do if we won the lottery. We all spend time wondering about life, the world, our children, what it will be like to have a better job, what our garden will look like in spring, what our house would look like if we painted it, and a myriad of other thoughts.

The Virgin Mary experienced things that probably felt unbelievable. Even she must have wondered at times, *is this happening to me?* The visit from the angel, the virgin birth, all of these people showing up to "worship" a newborn baby? How could this not be overwhelming?

I've shared with people many times that if I thought long enough and hard enough about what I'm doing as a priest, I'd probably run away in shame. After all, who am I to touch *the* Body of Christ at every Liturgy? Yet, someone has to do that. If you thought long enough and hard enough, you might run away from Holy Communion. After all, who are any of us to be receiving *the* Body and Blood of Christ? Yet, Christ calls us to receive Him.

In my own life, I find the more I ponder the things of God, the more convicted I feel in my faith, the more confident I feel in practicing my faith, the more confident and joyful I am to celebrate the Liturgy. During Holy Week, as an example, I feel so close to God and feel so much power coming from God because during that week in particular, so much of my time and thought is centered on God. I am *pondering* Him almost non-stop. At other times, when the Lord feels far away, when I think about it, I realize *my* thoughts of Him are far away. So, when I am pondering the things of God, when I am praying, when I am contemplating the things I say I believe, when I am engrossed in scripture, then my faith is growing and strong. When I do not do these things, then my faith is not as strong.

One of the reasons we worship at the Divine Liturgy each Sunday is to *remember* what Christ did for us. We go not only to receive Him in Communion, and not only to pray to Him, and to thank Him, but we go to *remember* Him and what He did for us. Before the Consecration of the Gifts, the priest prays:

> Remembering therefore this Divine Commandment of
> the Savior and all that came to pass for our sake, the cross,
> the tomb, the Resurrection on the third day, the Ascension

into heaven, and the enthronement and the right hand of the Father and the Second and Glorious coming. (From the Divine Liturgy of St. John Chrysostom, c/o Holy Cross Press)

We go to church in order to worship and in order to *ponder* on the things of God, to remember all that He has done for us, and all that is to come.

The Virgin Mary "kept these things and pondered them in her heart." She was careful with what she saw and did. She kept these special things in her heart, in the most special place. Remember many reflections back when we discussed having room in your heart for God. Well, one room in your heart should be the *pondering room*, a special place to store special thoughts of God that can be recalled at any moment, particularly at the tough moments in life. This is the place we store key verses of scripture, special moments we've shared with the Lord, so that when we are faced with a challenge, we have a place we can retreat for comfort and reassurance.

We spend so much of our life pandering—trying to get people to like us, dealing with peer pressure, trying to get people to "buy our product" (whatever idea or thing we are trying to convince people of), that we often forget to ponder on the things of God.

I'm reminded of the oft-quoted passage (attributed to Frank Outlaw):

Watch your thoughts. They become words.
Watch your words. They become deeds.
Watch your deeds. They become habit.
Watch your habits. They become character.
Character is everything.

To which I would add, watch your character, because this is what God is going to judge in order for anyone to inherit everlasting life.

The starting point of our character is our thought patterns. Fitting God into your thought pattern each day, keeping God's Word safely in your heart, pondering on the things of God in your mind—these things help us form good spiritual habits that shape our characters, which shape our lives, which prepare us for Eternal Life.

> Mary, why are you amazed and awed by what was done in you? And she answers, "For in time I have brought forth a timeless Son. But I have no understanding of His conception. Husbandless am I: How can I bear a son? Who has ever seen seedless childbirth? But where God wills, the order found in nature is overcome, as it is written." So Christ was born from the Virgin Maiden, in Bethlehem of Judea. (Kathisma from the Orthros of the Nativity. Trans. Fr. Seraphim Dedes)

Think about Christ today!

December 13

Something Has to Change

*And **the shepherds returned**, glorifying and praising God*
for all they had heard and seen, as it had been told them.
—Luke 2:20

I wonder if there was a moment when the shepherds, after all that they had heard and seen, sat down and said to themselves, "Wait, we're still just shepherds." Maybe they even had a moment of disappointment that their good spiritual fortune didn't translate into a change in financial fortune. Yes, after this miraculous experience of hearing angels and looking with their very own eyes on the Son of God now appearing in the flesh, they were still shepherds. They still had to return to the lonely and dangerous job of watching their flocks. They didn't move up the social ladder in society. They returned to their jobs as shepherds and materially, nothing changed.

Yet they were changed for the experience. For they had seen God. They had had an experience of God. And as they returned to their flocks, they were glorifying and praising God for what they had heard and seen. They were not lamenting to God why their material fortunes had not changed. They were praising God because their spiritual fortunes had changed. They were materially poor and that didn't change. They had been spiritually poor and now they were spiritually rich.

Becoming a Christian does not change ones socio-economic status. One can pray and have a profound experience of God and still remain poor, or sick, or unpopular, or any other undesirable status. Christians and non-Christians are just as likely to be a victim of a terrorist attack, or get struck by lightning, or catch a cold or have cancer. Having Christ doesn't make us immune to these things. Faith alone does not usually cure disease, that's why God gave people the talent to be doctors and nurses.

So, what does faith do? First, it gives us a destination. Faith in Christ focuses us for eternal life, not just life on earth. So, when life on earth gets difficult or disappointing, the person of faith consoles himself with the thought that this earthly life and its successes and failures are fleeting in the span on eternal life. The person of faith doesn't get too high on life's successes or low on its failures. The person of faith uses the tools of the faith—The Fruits of the Spirit (love, joy, peace, patience, kindness, goodness, faithfulness, gentleness, self-control—Gal. 5:22–23), gratitude, service, prayer, scripture, worship, sacraments—to arm one's soul with the tools to overcome adversity, pain, disappointment and failure. I firmly believe that having faith does not make one immune to life's disappointments, but gives us the strength to endure and overcome them, because faith focuses us on the forever, not the temporary.

Does my faith affect my material status? Yes, in a way it does. If I recognize a God-given talent, and I ask the Lord to help me develop that talent, and if I try to walk hand-in-hand with the Lord in using my talent, and that talent leads to a job that helps put food on my table and a roof over my head, then faith does in some way affect my material blessings as well. This is why when one is very materially blessed, for example an athlete who makes millions of dollars, it affords him an opportunity to make a witness for Christ, giving glory to God who has endowed him with athletic talents. And even if one isn't a millionaire, giving back to God from what He first gave us, offering gifts from His own gifts, is an important and crucial part of the Christian life. Whether you call it stewardship or tithing or just plain gratitude, giving back to God is something we should do generously and joyfully.

Moving back to the feast of Christmas, now only a few days away, what is going to change in your life after Christmas this year? I wonder the same thing after each year's Lenten journey. Does anything change just because we've sung some carols, put up decorations and heard the Christmas story yet again? I won't be any richer the day after Christmas. In fact when I tally up the credit card for the gifts I've bought for other people, there is a good chance I will be materially poorer. Christmas won't change the house I live in, or my son's grade in math.

Like the shepherds returned, once Christmas is over, our house will return to normal when we take the decorations down, our son will return to school, we'll return to work after a few days off and life will look almost exactly like it does today in a few weeks when all of this is over. If this is so, why celebrate Christmas at all? And, does it have to be like this?

One of the reasons why we celebrate feasts like the Nativity on a yearly basis is to remember what the Lord did for us. As we get older, hopefully we come to a deeper understanding of what the Nativity really means. Your participation in reading these reflections is hopefully leading you to a deeper understanding of not only the Nativity but of the Christian faith. My writing them is helping me do that. As I ponder on the shepherds returning to their flocks and their hum-drum lives, but profoundly changed for the experience, I am thinking of ways that I can let my Christian faith change my life, how can I return glorifying and praising God once Christmas has passed. In some sense, today's verse is the most important verse of the Nativity scriptures, because if we do not allow the experience of God to change us, then we are merely going through yearly rituals throughout our lives in a way that is almost pointless. The endpoint of our Christian life is supposed to be an entrance into the Kingdom of Heaven. Yearly milestones of holidays, and even daily mileposts, are supposed to be occasions when we peel back another layer of God's mysteries, promises, and beauty, so that we come to a deeper understanding of God and so that we "return glorifying and praising God" on an ever deepening level.

The shepherds were still shepherds after their encounter with Christ. But they had changed. They heard the angels, they went with haste to find Christ, they told others what they had experienced. They demonstrated faith, and faith brought them joy, and joy is what led them to glorify and praise God with happiness and purpose, even as they returned to being shepherds.

We must seek to do the same—we must hear the message, we must go and be doers and not just hearers, and we must be encouragers. When we do these things, we will find not only faith but joy. Joy is what will help us glorify and praise God with happiness and purpose, even as we return each day to the material challenges we all face.

> Direct my steps according to Your teaching and let no lawlessness rule over me. Ransom me from the slander of men, and I will keep Your commandments. Make Your face shine upon Your servant and teach me Your ordinances. Let my mouth be filled with Your praise, O Lord, that I may sing of Your glory and of Your magnificence all the day long. (Prayer from the Royal Hours of Nativity. Trans. Fr. Seraphim Dedes)

Return with joy to work, school, home, and whatever else you return to today!

December 14

Leaving and Following

*Now when Jesus was born in Bethlehem of Judea in the days of Herod the king, behold, **wise men came** from the East to Jerusalem, saying "Where is he who has been born king of the Jews? For we have seen His star in the East and have come to worship Him."*
—Matthew 2:1–2

Today we leave the account of the shepherds and shift to the visit of the Magi. Only the Gospels of Matthew and Luke contain the narrative of the Nativity. Luke focuses on the angels and shepherds, while Matthew focuses on the Magi.

So, who were the Magi, and what do we know about them?

We know that they were "from the East," but their exact country is not specified. It is possible that they came from different countries, so we cannot conclude that they came together, or that there were even three of them.

Three gifts have been identified—gold, frankincense, and myrrh—as having been offered by the Magi. This has led to the tradition that there were THREE Magi, though the number three is not mentioned in the Bible. In fact, the Syriac Orthodox tradition hold that there were twelve Magi.

These men are referred to as three kings, wise men, and Magi. In Greek, they are referred to exclusively as *Mayoi* or "Magi" in English. We cannot conclude conclusively whether they were rulers, or scientists, or scholars. Some historians consider the Magi as members of an eastern religious cult who were converted through a star. Others hold that they were astrologers who had knowledge of a bright star that would appear to announce the birth of the Christ.

The Magi have been given names in some Christian traditions: Melchior, a Persian scholar; Caspar (or Gaspar), an Indian scholar; and Balthazar, a Babylonian scholar. In other traditions, Melchior is depicted as a king of Persia, Gaspar as a king of India and Balthazar as a king of Arabia. The Magi, in art and iconography, are also depicted as being of different ages. Caspar is old, shown with a long, white beard, and he gives the gift of gold. Melchior is shown as middle-aged, with a short brown beard, and brings incense. Balthazar is depicted as a young man without a beard who brings myrrh. In some portrayals, Balthazar is shown with dark skin, leading to tradition that he came from Ethiopia or another part of Africa.

As you can see, there are many traditions that have sprung up around the Magi. What the Bible says conclusively is that wise men came from far away and brought gifts to the Christ. They followed a star in order to find Christ. When they found Him, they worshipped Him.

Whether they left kingdoms, or philosophy positions, or were religious leaders who left their temples, whether there were three of them or many more, and whether they came from one part of the world or several places, what is most important about the Magi is that they *left* and *followed* until they found the Christ. They left their cities, the comforts of home and set out across deserts and mountains, undoubtedly enduring hardships along the way.

We are called to do the same—to leave and to follow. For the Magi, the leaving was a physical leaving from a location, and walking or riding on camel (the traditional animal they are shown to travel on, but the Bible isn't specific about that either); going to a faraway land over the course of two years. They didn't know where they were going or how long it would take to get there but they followed.

For us, following Christ does not necessarily involve uprooting and leaving your house and going to another city. It does, however, involve leaving certain tendencies that we all have. We all have a tendency to be angry, greedy, ungrateful, egotistical, jealous, unforgiving, slanderous, prideful and selfish. So, if we are to truly follow Christ, we need to "leave" these things and follow His commandments.

The Magi were also *seekers*. They weren't sure exactly who or what they were going to find, they just kept following the star. We also must be seekers. As with the Magi, the Christianity does have an element of FAITH, trust in the unknown or not fully known. The Bible says "Seek and you shall find (Matt. 7:7)." But we will not find anything without seeking.

Leaving, following, and seeking are what lead to finding. It led the Magi to find Christ. May it lead us to do the same.

> O Savior, You were secretly born in the cave, but heaven used the star as a mouth and announced You to all. It brought to You the Magi who worshipped You with faith. Together with them have mercy on us. (From the Vespers of the Nativity. Trans. Fr. Seraphim Dedes)

Seek after God today!

December 15

Come to the Dark Side—uh, NO!!!

*When **Herod the king heard this, he was troubled, and all of Jerusalem***
***with him;** and assembling all the chief priests and scribes of the people,*
he inquired of them where the Christ was to be born. They told him, "In
Bethlehem of Judea; for so it is written by the prophet:
'And you, O Bethlehem, in the land of Judah, are by no means least
among the rulers of Judah; for from you shall come a ruler
who will govern my people Israel.'"
—Matthew 2:3–6

I guess every good story has its villain, and in the Nativity story that "villain" is King Herod. The Magi had just come to his palace after a long journey, eager to find the "king" they had been searching for. Herod, however, did not share their joy. He was "troubled, and all of Jerusalem with him." (Mt. 2:2) After all, was this new "king" going to be a threat to his rule and the rule of the Romans over the Jews? He then assembled the chief priests and scribes from the Jewish temple and grilled them about where the Christ was to be born. Even the Jewish temple leadership, those who served as "kings" over the Jews, and who you would have thought would be happy at the prospect of a king to deliver them from their Roman overlords, had to have been troubled by this news. There had to have been some collusion between Roman and Jewish leaders that this new "King of the Jews" was not going to be good for any of them. Herod would shortly order the deaths of all male children under age two in the area, so scared was he of a baby boy who might one day overthrow him. And thirty years later, the chief priests and scribes of the Jews would conspire to kill Christ and succeed—well for three days anyway.

There are a lot of "King Herods" in the world today, people who misunderstand who Christ is and count Him, the King of Peace, as an enemy. They hate the One who personifies love.

It always perplexes me how people could be up in arms with the Ten Commandments being placed on the wall of a courthouse. Not only are they the foundation of Western law, but how can people object to the ideas of "thou shalt not steal," or "thou shalt not commit murder?" People get angry at Christmas tree displays. I understand getting angry at people, but I've never gotten angry at a tree. The name *Christmas* itself gets bad press. Ironically, I'm more likely to wish someone a "blessed Nativity" than a "Merry Christmas"—I wonder which is more offensive.

The world has turned Christmas into a holiday of material gain. Commercialism is ruining the season. Stress has overtaken joy. "King Herod" and his cohorts are still trying to ruin Christmas.

So, if we are supposed to be seekers like the Magi, and if we are supposed to be trusting like the Magi, then we have to be focused like the Magi. The Magi were undeterred by the plotting of King Herod. They kept their focus only on finding Christ. And once they found Him, they stayed away from Herod. Not wanting to betray the Savior they had come to know, they went back to their country by a different way.

Sometimes it seems like the easier thing to do to just give in to the crowd, rather than do what feels like paddling upstream. It's easier just to go to the parties than maintain a Nativity fast. It's easier to just say "Happy Holidays" than risk offending someone with "Merry Christmas." It's easier to let the darkness of this season cover up the Light of Christ. No one, however, said that being a Christian would be easy. The hero in any story always has to overcome adversity and defeat the villain. Jesus tells us in Matthew 5:14–16:

> You are the light of the world. A city set on a hill cannot be hid. Nor do men light a lamp and put it under a bushel, but on a stand, and it gives light to all in the house. Let your light so shine before men, that they may see your good works and give glory to your Father who is in heaven.

One of the responsibilities of the Christian is to be a light in the world, and that's not always easy to do.

If the feast of the Nativity is about the presence of Christ the Light coming into the world, even the placement of the feast on the calendar has to do with light. No one knows the date of the Nativity. The date of the crucifixion has been traced the 13th day of the Jewish month of Nissan, right before Passover. So we know that the crucifixion occurred in the spring. We do not know what season the Nativity occurred in. We know that the Nativity occurred somewhere between 6 and 4 B.C. based on when King Herod died, which was shortly after the slaughter of the Innocents, which occurred two years after the Nativity.

The feast of the Nativity was placed in December in the year 336 A.D. There were other holidays celebrated at this time of year including the pagan feast of the solstice, or the shortest day of the year. Whether the Nativity was placed on December 25 in order to compete with the pagan holiday, or because other holidays were celebrated at that time of year in society—hence the *holiday season*—what is a beautiful symbolism is that after the solstice, December 21, the days begin to get longer, the light begins to overtake the darkness. Through the Nativity, the Light of Christ begins to overcome the darkness of sin.

As we prepare to celebrate the Nativity, we must think of the "lightness" of the shepherds and the Magi. The shepherds were poor, the Magi were powerful, but both were filled with the Light of Christ because both had faith. Herod and his court were filled with the darkness of jealousy and power. We must resist the urge to go to the dark side and remain in the Light of Christ. We must stand up for what we believe in. For the Lord blesses those who praise Him and sanctifies those who put their trust in Him (from the Liturgy of St. John Chrysostom, c/o Holy Cross Press). There are lots of roles in the Nativity story for us to imitate—Mary, Joseph, the shepherds, the Magi—King Herod is the one role we should not want to play.

O Christ, the true Light that enlightens and sanctifies every man who comes into the world, let the light of Your countenance shine on us, that in it we may behold the unapproachable Light. And direct our steps to keep Your commandments, by the intercessions of Your all-immaculate Mother and all the saints. Amen. (Prayer of the First Hour, from the Royal Hours. Trans. Fr. Seraphim Dedes)

Let your Light shine today!

December 16

This journey is a long one

Then Herod summoned the wise men secretly and ascertained from them
what time the star appeared*; and he sent them to Bethlehem, saying*
"Go and search diligently for the Child, and when you have found Him
bring me word, that I too may come and worship Him."
—Matthew 2:3–8

The Bible has fixed the length of the journey of the Magi as being just under two years. When they arrived at the palace of King Herod, he secretly ascertained from them what time the star appeared. Herod felt threatened by the idea of a "King of the Jews" who could threaten his reign over the land. After the visit of the Magi, when they went back to their country without telling Herod the whereabouts of the Christ-child, Herod "was in a furious rage, and he sent and killed all the male children in Bethlehem and in all that region who were **two years old or under**, according to the time he had ascertained from the wise men (Matt. 2:16)."

It was just under a two—year journey from the time the star appeared until the Magi appeared in Bethlehem and found Christ. In Matthew 2:11, it says: "and going into the house they saw the Child with Mary His Mother." Unlike the traditional manger scenes that show shepherds and Magi arriving at the same time on Christmas night, it was only the shepherds that went to the cave and worshipped at the manger. The Magi worshipped Christ as a *Child*, not as a baby. They met Him in a house, not at the cave.

It's hard to imagine what it would be like to walk across the United States. That seems like it would be a difficult task. It is made easier because we have paved roads, milepost markers, and GPS to tell us where we are at all times and how far we have to go and to keep us from getting lost. There are restaurants where we can find food, hotels to find shelter, and most importantly, a finite destination. You know that in 3,000 miles you are going to hit the ocean. So, walking five miles a day, it would take you less than two years. Parts of India are, in fact, 3,000 miles from Bethlehem. So, a five-mile-a-day pace might have been the speed of the Magi.

Now imagine you took that walk across America without the benefit of a road, with no road-side hotels and restaurants, with only the sun to guide you by day and the stars to guide you at night. While a five mile walk on a paved road might not seem like that big of a deal, how about crossing the Rocky Mountains without a road in the middle of winter?! You wouldn't be moving at five miles a day for sure! And most challenging of all, imagine that you started walking across America without knowing how far it is across America, or what is on the other side—you just walk, and walk, and walk, wondering if it will ever end, and wondering even HOW it will end and WHERE.

This was the journey of the Magi—as the popular carol says "field and fountain, moor and mountain, following yonder star." This was a journey of faith and trust, patience and perseverance, for nearly two long years.

The journey of the Magi in many ways mirrors the journey of the Christian life. We have our "star." We believe that it leads somewhere special, which is eternal life. But the journey is long. We don't have mile markers and sign posts to tell us how close we are or how far we still have to go, just like the Magi didn't. The journey is fraught with hardships. Just like the Magi must have endured bad weather, we too must endure "storms" in life. Just like the Magi had to leave creature comforts they probably missed, so we also must leave behind certain comforts that are not in line with Christianity and just follow. I'm sure there were days that the Magi wondered if they would ever reach their destination, where they didn't make much progress, where they wondered if they were going in the right direction, and there were probably days when they realized they had taken a wrong turn and backtracked. All of these things are part of the Christian journey. But just like the journey of the Magi, we believe our journey will end with us beholding Christ with our own eyes.

I've heard it said that "80 percent of life is just showing up." And that's true. When you don't show up, nothing can happen. But when you show up, that's when things happen. I often think as I watch especially the older members of our church, who have been coming for decade after decade to this church, and wonder, "do they ever get tired of the Christian journey?" While I'm sure that they all do, just like I do at times, they keep showing up, they keep putting one foot in front of the other so to speak and making progress towards the star which shines over the ultimate destination, the Kingdom of Heaven. I may not make progress every day, or at every service or in every prayer. Sometimes I just show up with my body but not my mind. However, over time, I feel like I am making progress in my journey. And I hope you feel the same way about your own journey.

If your journey is going well, keep your eyes on the star. If your journey is not going as well as you'd like, make sure you keep your eyes on the star. And if your journey isn't going well, get your eyes back on the star. And keep walking, keep moving, keep following, keep showing up, keep trying. And most especially find other "Magi;" others who are following the star, so that they can encourage and support you in your journey, and you can support and encourage them in theirs.

Ours is not a star that leads to nowhere, but a star that leads to Christ, in the Kingdom of Heaven.

> Teach me Thy way, O Lord, that I may walk in Thy truth; unite my heart to fear Thy name. I will give thanks to Thee, O Lord my God, with my whole heart, and I will glorify Thy name forever. For great is Thy steadfast love towards me . . . Show me a sign of Thy favor, that those who hate me may see and be put to shame, because Thou, Lord, hast helped me and comforted me. (Psalm 86:11–13, 17. Read at the Royal Hours of the Nativity)

Keep on walking!

December 17

All Signs Point in One Direction

*When they had heard the king they went their way; and lo, **the star***
*which they had seen in the East **went before them**, till it came to rest over*
the place where the child was. When they saw the star,
***they rejoiced exceedingly** with great joy.*
—Matthew 2:9–10

$\mathcal{E}$very year when I go to summer camp, I try to spend an hour on one of the nights that I am there laying on my back and staring up at the stars. This is something that I can't do in Tampa (where I live), because the bright city lights do not allow for good viewing of the stars. In fact, if someone grew up in Tampa, or another big city, and never got out into the country, it would be hard for them to even understand what a star is, or know that there are literally millions of them. Yet, when you go out into the country, away from the busy city, the amount of stars in the sky on a clear night is overwhelmingly beautiful and powerful. I'm always reminded of the verses of Psalm 147: "He determines the number of the stars, He gives to all of them their names. Great is our Lord, and abundant in power (Ps. 147:4–5)." This experience of the stars—one insignificant person laying out under the blanket of the heavens—always reinforces for me that there is a power much greater than any of us at work among us, and that power is none other than God. This experience takes one back to the first thing needed to have faith, the first sign, which is that someone greater than us made us.

The Magi were guided by a star. They kept it in front of them at all times. They rejoiced when they saw it. They kept their eyes on the prize, the star that directed their journey, from its beginning to its ultimate destination.

As I mentioned in the last reflection, the "star shines over the destination." It provided the Magi the direction to their ultimate destination. In the Nativity narrative, that destination was a home where Christ was. For us, the destination is our salvation, the Kingdom of Heaven. And our "star," if you will, is the *Cup of Salvation*—Holy Communion.

During the Stanley Cup hockey playoffs, there are endless advertisements which say "It's all about the Cup!" And indeed, for the Christian, it is all about the Cup. The central act of the church is partaking of the Cup of Salvation, touching the Divine God through the Eucharist. Take the Cup out of the church and you have no church. The Church exists to share the Cup and to bring as many people as possible to it. Ideally, our entire life should revolve around the Cup—we should either be partaking of the Cup (Sundays, and other days when it is offered), or thanking God for the Eucharist, or preparing to receive Christ in the Eucharist. Our whole life should revolve around that. Our identity as Christians should begin and end with the Cup.

For the Magi, the journey was about the Star. When they saw the Star, they rejoiced. Whichever way the Star led, they followed. They didn't exactly know where the star was leading, but wherever it was leading, they were happy to follow. The Bible doesn't tell us if they ever became angry because the journey was taking so long, or doubtful of where it was going. To be sure, they must have had moments of anger and moments of doubt. The most joyful journeys in our lives have both—think marriage and having children. But the primary emotion of the Magi was joy at the Star that was ever the focal point of their journey.

For us, the contemporary Christians, our star is the Cup of Salvation. Does that mean that we never get angry or frustrated, especially at the Lord? No, we can have moments of frustration, even with the Lord. Does the Cup as our focal point mean that we never have a moment of doubt? Certainly not, we can have moments of doubt. But the primary emotion we want as Christians is JOY, and the joy comes from the Lord, and it is fed by the Cup. Every night, the Magi came back to that star and that kept them going. In the same way, we are supposed to come to the Cup each Sunday, that is supposed to be our guide and guardian, what sustains and inspires us.

I love what it is written in Isaiah 40:26: "Lift up your eyes on high and see: who created these? He who brings out their host by number, calling them all by name; by the greatness of His might, and because He is strong in power, not one is missing." Yes, that counts for stars. But it also counts for souls!

The Magi found joy even in the celestial signs, even though Christ wasn't fully revealed to them and they didn't have full understanding of Him. May this serve as an example for us to do the same. Faith is believing without fully knowing or fully comprehending. May we have the perseverance of the Magi as we make our journey of faith, keeping our eyes on our "star."

At the Nativity, for the Magi on their long journey, it was all about the Star. All of their faith and energy was put in that one direction!

As we prepare to celebrate the Nativity this year, and for eternal life, we have to make it all about the Cup. This is our star, our sign, and our faith and energy needs to go in that one direction!

The wise men concluded from their observations of the extraordinary path of the peculiar nova which had lately appeared and was shining more brightly than anything in outer space, that Christ the King was born on earth, in Bethlehem to save our souls. (9th Ode, Orthros of the Nativity. Trans. Fr. Seraphim Dedes)

Walk in one (God's) direction today!

December 18

I Can Only Imagine

And going into the house they saw the child with Mary His mother,
*and **they fell down and worshipped Him**.*
—Matthew 2:11

What would your first reaction be if you walked into a room and Christ was there? One can only imagine the scene when the Magi walked into the house where Jesus was, when they opened the door and laid their eyes on the reason that they had left home and followed a star for two years. They fell down and they worshipped Him. They must have had feelings of joy and awe, and probably also humility and unworthiness.

What will it be like the first time we cast our gaze on our Creator? We will all see God face-to-face at the Last Judgment. I remember hearing once that those who are not destined to be forever with God, those who are headed toward eternal condemnation, will not need to wait to hear that they are condemned. They will see the face of God and know that they have no business being with God because their earthly lives will not have reflected the preparation needed to enter eternal life. They will know this, they will not need for God to tell them. On the other hand, those who have prepared for eternal life in this life, will gaze upon the face of God with joy. It will be the triumphant end of a long journey. Just like the Magi traveled over deserts and mountains for two years, trusting in a star, that it would lead them somewhere magnificent, those who travel the journey of life with their eyes on Christ will experience the joy of the Magi when God opens the gates of heaven for them.

Many people still don't understand the concept of worship. Many think that worship is only paying homage to God, even giving Him His due. Worship is so much more than this.

Worship is learning. We learn about God through worship. As we sing hymns about the Lord, and hear Scripture passages and sermons, we learn about the Lord.

Worship helps us remember. We are bombarded with all kinds of information and stimulation in the world that it is easy to forget what God did for us. One of the reasons we worship is to remember what Jesus did for us in coming to earth to teach us, heal us, and ultimately to die for our sins.

Worship provides a good support group. Can you imagine a solitary wise man following a star for two years? I can imagine a group of wise men following the star, and occasionally one becoming discouraged in the journey and being encouraged by the others to continue. It's hard to imagine how one person could make the journey of the wise men alone. It would not only be dangerous, but lonely. But for two years, to have no one to talk to about the journey, to have no one to offer encouragement, could the journey even have been made by one solitary man on a camel? Could this person maintain his enthusiasm, even sanity, without someone to help and encourage him? Because God made us in His image and like-ness, we crave to be in union with others. Just as God exists in Trinity, we crave to exist in unity with others. Worship helps in this regard. Worship helps us to find encouragement in our faith because we are sharing the journey with others.

Worship offers us the opportunity to commune with God. There is no such thing as a private Communion. Communion by its very definition requires that it be shared. In the context of worship, we are able to share in Holy Communion with one another. Even when I am visiting someone who is sick, and it is just two of us, I am able to offer Communion in the context of two people worshipping God.

Worship affords us the opportunity to stand with God, to come to God in His house. When we worship, we step out of the world temporarily and we enter into the Kingdom of God, made present on earth.

Worship puts us in the role of the Magi. As we open the door to God's house, we gaze in wonder on God Himself, in the sacrament of Holy Communion. We stand with God, together with the saints and the angels and one another. I heard a priest once say that if we understood fully what we are doing in worship, that we stand in the presence of God, that people would come to church and fall flat on their faces in awe.

The Magi made a long journey to the Christ, but when the star came to rest over the place where He was, they opened the door, beheld the Lord with their own eyes and fell down and worshipped Him.

Each week, we endure a difficult journey of life. Each Sunday, we are supposed to come to the house where Christ is, with Mary, His Mother, and all the saints, and we are supposed to walk in the door and fall down and worship Him. Today's verse about the arrival of the Magi is something we should be experiencing on a weekly basis.

May the same faith and trust that sustained them in their journey to Christ sustain us in our journeys. And may the same awe that they felt when they laid their eyes on Him, that caused them to fall down and worship Him, may that same awe come upon us in our journeys, that we too may fall down and worship Him, and that we may one day have the doors of heaven opened to us so we can gaze upon Him with our own eyes.

You rose from the Virgin O Christ, the noetic Sun of Righteousness, and a star pointed to You, the Uncontainable contained in a cave. It led the Magi to worship You; and with them we magnify You. O Giver of Life, glory to You! (From Vespers of the Nativity. Trans. Fr. Seraphim Dedes)

Leave time for worship this (and every) week!

December 19

What Is a Gift?

Then opening their treasures, they offered Him gifts—
gold, frankincense and myrrh.
—Matthew 2:11

It seems that gift giving, for many, has become the center-piece of the Christmas holiday. Gifts have also become the greatest source of stress during the Christmas season. We stress about trying to find the perfect for everyone. It is stressful trying to find a parking space at the mall in order to buy gifts. We stress about how much time it takes to shop. We wonder whether the person will even like the gift we are buying. Then we stress out about how we will pay for all the gifts. People who receive lots of gifts stress about where to put them. People even stress about getting thank-you cards out. If two people exchange gifts and one person gives an expensive gift while the other one buys a less expensive gift, this could cause a friendship to be scarred. So there is stress even in exchanging gifts.

The tradition of giving gifts at Christmas comes from the visit of the Magi, who brought gifts to Christ. This has led to an almost near-obsession with gifts being associated with this important holiday. The local mall doesn't have a banner extolling the Nativity of Christ, but a running clock of days and hours until the end of the Christmas shopping season. As you read this message this morning, you're probably already keenly aware that there are only six shopping days left.

Think about all the stress surrounding the Nativity of Christ—a pregnant virgin, an unsure Joseph, no room at any inn, an overpopulation in Bethlehem, the dangers of the fields, the fear caused by the angel, the uncertainty of the shepherds, the anger of King Herod, and the long journey of the Magi. The LEAST stressful part of the first Christmas was the offering (notice I did not say exchanging, come back tomorrow to read about that) of gifts from the Magi to Christ.

Most people think a gift requires an outlay of money. The most meaningful gifts, if you think about it, cost no money. I can't tell you how many teens I've met at summer camp over the years who have told me "My parents buy me whatever I want, I just wish they would spend more time with me." I can't tell you how many times when people have asked me what do I want for Christmas, I tell them either I need some help in my ministry, or for any gesture that will lessen my stress. The hardest gift to give is not an expensive gift. The hardest gift to give is usually the gift of time, or a sympathetic ear, or a heartfelt letter. That's why when someone offers me either, these are the gifts I treasure most of all.

You don't have to spend a lot of money to give a great gift. If our son writes me a note saying "My gift to you this Christmas is a pledge to clean my room daily and not need reminders to do my homework," that would be a great gift. Can you imagine a husband and wife exchanging notes which say: "To my dear wife, I promise I'll remember to pick up my socks" and "To my dear husband, I promise I'll pick them up without nagging when you forget." Again, think about it, the best gifts are not the ones that cost the most money. These may, in fact, be the easiest gifts, because they don't require emotion or vulnerability.

You've still got six days left to shop for Christmas. Think of some non-material gifts you can give to those you love. A letter telling them what they mean to you. A pledge to improve some area of a relationship.

Forgiveness for a past offense. These are meaningful gifts that never wear out and never need to be replaced.

Whatever gift you offer, whether it is a material gift or a non-material gift, requires sacrifice. There is not gift that doesn't involve sacrifice. And when you make a sacrifice, you are supposed to do it with joy. When a person makes a giving gesture to someone else, they are not supposed to brag (or lament) what it cost them: "Look, I bought this expensive gift for you," or "Look what I sacrificed for you." That kind of giving creates either an obligation to give a gift in return, or guilt for accepting the gift, or both. So, whatever you are giving, give with joy. Focus on the joy of giving, not the sacrifice. Allow the receiver of the gift to accept it with joy and without any guilt.

And there is no such thing as self-sacrifice. You can't take from yourself and turn around and give right back to yourself. That is self-serving. So when you decide you want to buy a gift for yourself, it is really not a gift. You are going to buy something for yourself, but you can't call it a gift. A gift is divesting yourself of something—either money, or time, or emotion—and imparting that to someone else.

> Heaven called the Magi by a star, and thus it brought the first-fruits of Gentiles to You, the infant lying in the manger. And they were amazed, not by scepters and thrones, but by the utter poverty. For what is more shabby than a cave? And what is more humble than swaddling clothes? But it was through these that the riches of Your Divinity shone forth. Lord, glory to You! (Hypakoe from the Orthros of the Nativity. Trans. Fr. Seraphim Dedes)

Give with joy today!

December 20

Are You "Giving" or "Exchanging"?

*Then opening their treasures, **they offered Him gifts**—*
gold, frankincense and myrrh.
—Matthew 2:11

Many workplaces make a gift exchange part of their office Christmas party. This is done so that everyone brings one gift and receives one gift and it insures that everyone only has to buy one and everyone gets to receive one.

When you think about it, a *gift exchange* is a conflict in terms. For the true gift is the gift that is given, not the gift that is exchanged. To give something means to divest oneself of something, offering it to someone else without expecting anything in return. In other words, a true gift is offered, not given, and it is offered without any expectations and without any strings attached. That's why in the church context, a gift given with strings attached, or expectations, really cannot be considered a gift—it is an exchange. When people get mad at the church or the priest and withhold their gifts, it always makes me wonder were those really gifts to begin with?

The Magi traveled for two years in order to meet Christ. That in itself was a gift of time. They offered Him treasures, things that had material value. While the material value of a gift is not necessarily what makes a good gift, one cannot offer a gift that costs nothing—no time, no sacrifice of something.

The Magi didn't burst through the door of the house, rush to Jesus, offer Him their gifts and then ask "Where are our gifts?" And despite the fact that there was no exchange of material gifts, the Magi did not leave the house disappointed because they brought in gifts and didn't depart with any.

On the contrary, the Magi did receive a gift. For beneath the star they had followed for two years lay the greatest gift of all, the Son of God in the flesh. With their own eyes, they saw God made man, heaven come to earth, what greater gift can there be?

It seems in some sense that we have become greedy, because we measure everything in material terms. We don't always see immaterial things as gifts. We don't appropriately treasure the gift of a new day, the fact that we are all still living and breathing today. Or the fact that the sun came out to give warmth and promote the growth of plants. People have often lamented "Why should I give to God? He hasn't given to me." To which I always think *The most precious thing we have is life itself. Because without life, what good is anything that we have, including our families? We can only enjoy our families while we are alive. So the very fact that God has given each of us a gift of a new day, to do whatever you plan to do today, is a great gift He has given to us, the gift of life itself, the gift of a new day.*

Some people on Christmas will lament their gifts—they will be sad that they "didn't get what I really wanted." And then they will go and return the gifts and get something else with the money. Some of this behavior, I suppose, is understandable—if you get two of the same thing, I guess you return the one you don't need. Ideally, as Jesus says in Luke 3:11, "He who has two coats, let him share with him who has none." That is the ideal. There are some gifts, again I suppose, that we cannot use. I do not play golf, so if someone sent me a set of golf clubs for Christmas, for instance, I would probably exchange them for something I really need but can't afford. But I can't say I recall lamenting a material gift.

We do tend to lament spiritual gifts, or rather our perceived lack of them, at times. We wonder why others have been blessed, or at least we perceive that they are blessed, and why we are not as blessed? However, as St. Paul writes in Ephesians 4:7, "grace was given to EACH of us, according to the measure of Christ's gift." Each of us has some manifestation of Christ's grace in us. This comes out in our personalities and our talents. There is no one who has no gift to offer the world, or who has no gift to offer back to Christ. Because we are ALL made in the image and likeness of God, then everyone has infinite value in the eyes of God. So, while our gifts and talents may be different, God doesn't value anyone more or less than anyone else—we all have infinite value in His eyes.

Because God so freely gives to us, we are to freely give to one another. When you give with strings attached, or expecting something in return, then you are "exchanging," not "giving." And there is an important difference.

Many people try to exchange gifts with God. They make deals with God. "I will give more money to the church, but I hope for a better seat in heaven." As if there is preferred seating in heaven. Just to get to heaven shows that you are preferred. And there is the more common "I'll make You a deal God—get me out of this jam that I'm in and I'll give my life to you, or at least make a few changes in it." Again, this is an exchange.

Christ gave us the par excellence example of offering a gift when He offered Himself on the Cross for our sins. He didn't ask for anything in return. He didn't demand anything in return. He didn't try to cut a deal with God. He went to His death on the cross saying, "Father, into Thy hands I commit My Spirit (Luke 23:46)!" He didn't go to His death asking God for a deal. To the contrary He said, "Father, if Thou art willing, remove this cup from me; nevertheless, not My Will, but Thine, be done (John 22:42)."

And because Christ has shown us the example of how to truly give a gift, by giving His very life for us, we should also learn what it is to give, not only in how we give to God but how we give to one another. We should be willing to give to our neighbor without expectation of reward or return.

We've all heard the saying "It is more blessed to give than to receive." As we go through this Christmas season, as the time of gift-giving is upon us, focus on your giving of gifts to other people, rather than the gifts you will receive. The best gifts in life really are the ones that you give, just for the joy of giving, expecting nothing in return.

> Today in Bethlehem, Christ is born of the Virgin. Today, the Unoriginate begins, and the Word becomes flesh. The hosts of heaven are rejoicing, and the earth and humanity are merry. The Magi bring their gifts. The Shepherds proclaim the marvel. And we unceasingly cry aloud: "Glory to God in the highest, and on earth, peace, goodwill toward men!" (The Praises, Orthros of the Nativity. Trans. Fr. Seraphim Dedes)

Look for ways to give to people today!

December 21

Meaningful Gifts

Then opening their treasures, they offered Him gifts—
gold, frankincense and myrrh.
—Matthew 2:11

The Magi did not come empty-handed to visit the Christ-child. They brought Him treasures, gifts that they considered valuable, gifts that befit the "King" they were coming to visit. They presumably brought these treasures from their homelands. There wasn't a Walmart or a mall in Bethlehem. So they had not only the burden of purchasing a gift, they had the burden of transporting and safeguarding the treasures they were carrying. These gifts were going to be special gifts indeed.

These gifts were carefully selected with Christ in mind, gifts that befit a king. The gifts they offered were three:

Gold—From nearly the beginning of time, gold and precious metals have held great value. This is why kings wear a gold crown, as a sign of their kingship, their authority, their power. Gold is representative of Christ's Kingship on earth.

Frankincense—Incense was burned in the temple, and is a sign of divinity. The Magi were the first to recognize the divinity of Christ in presenting Him with this gift.

Myrrh—The purpose of Christ coming to earth was to die for our sins. Remember the swaddling clothes, the burial bands which prefigured the burial of Christ? Myrrh was used with other spices in anointing the bodies of the dead to prepare them for burial. Myrrh is presented to Christ prefiguring His death and burial for our sakes.

When we offer gifts, whether to God or to one another, we should follow the example of the Magi. We should offer gifts that are meaningful. The gifts offered to the Christ-child represented material things (gold), spiritual things (incense), and purposeful things (myrrh). These provide good parameters in our giving of gifts to each other, and especially to God.

Let's discuss our gifts to one another. We should give to one another in a material way, whether this is an outlay of resources to buy a gift, or an outlay of time to assist each other in some way. This is the "gold" we give to one another.

We should give to one another in a spiritual way. The gift of prayer is something that we can't put a price on. It is even more valuable than gold. After all, what could be a greater gift to offer someone than speaking to our God about him or her? When someone says to me "I pray for you every day," that is the greatest gift of all, the greatest possible gift I can receive. Prayer is the "frankincense" we can offer each other.

Without a purpose, there is no point to anything. Without a purpose to this life, there is no point to it. The purpose in this life is to reach everlasting life. Thus the purpose of every marriage is mutual salvation. That is also the ultimate purpose of every close friendship. That doesn't mean we need to make the basis of every conversation, every outing to a sports event, and every meal we share a discussion on spiritual things. But it means that cultivating things like the fruits of the Spirit in our relationships is important, because it is ultimately these fruits and other spiritual things that lead us to our ultimate destination, salvation. When you offer forgiveness, this restores love. When you offer encouragement to others, this leads them to a greater sense of joy. When you help others reduce stress, this promotes peace. When you aren't always nagging, that promotes patience. When you do things without being asked, that promotes kindness. When you are optimistic, that promotes goodness. When you are humble, that promotes gentleness. When you put Christ at the center of a relationship, this promotes faithfulness. And when you don't tempt people or goad them into gossip or other unhealthy choices, this promotes self-control. Offer any of these gifts to anybody and these gifts of purpose will not only grow a friendship or a marriage, but the will help get closer to our ultimate purpose, salvation. Purposeful gifts are the "myrrh" we can offer each other.

> Lord, I have cried to You; hear me. Hear me O Lord. Lord, I have cried out to You; hear me. Give heed to the voice of my supplication when I cry to You. Hear me, O Lord.
>
> Let my prayer be set forth before You as incense, the lifting up of my hands as the evening sacrifice. Hear me, O Lord. (Sung at the Vespers of the Nativity. Trans. Fr. Seraphim Dedes)

Make sure you are "wrapping" some *spiritual* and *purposeful* gifts to give away this Christmas!

December 22

I Have No Gift to Bring!

Wait. There Is Exactly ONE Gift I CAN Bring!

*Then opening their treasures, they offered Him **gifts**—*
gold, frankincense and myrrh.
—Matthew 2:11

As we run around purchasing, wrapping, and delivering gifts for other people this Christmas, we must ask ourselves seriously and soberly, "What gift am I offering to Him this Christmas?" As we are now in the home stretch heading towards the Feast of the Nativity as we count down now the hours until we are at the manger, we have to consider what gift we will bring to Christ at the Nativity. I have always liked the Christmas carol, "The Little Drummer Boy." I especially love the line "I have no gift to bring . . . that's fit to give a king . . . shall I play for you . . . on my drum?" The realization that he has no material gift to bring—but that he has the gift of himself, his talent to offer—is so beautiful. The Little Drummer Boy feels almost sad at his meager gift. The baby Jesus receives this gift with joy: "Then He smiled at me." And then the Little Drummer Boy realizes that his gift was acceptable to Christ, because it was the gift of himself.

When you think about it, what gift do we really have to give to Christ this Christmas? We really have NOTHING to give. We only have things that we can GIVE BACK. Because everything we have that is good is from

Him. The money that I have that I am using to buy gifts comes as a result of my having a job. My having a job comes as a result of my having a talent. And my having a talent comes as a result of being blessed by God with that talent. Anything I have that is good has God at its origin.

There are things I can give *to other people.* I can only GIVE BACK to God. So, when I am giving to charity, either to the church or to some charity; I am really giving back to God. He has blessed me with material resources and in giving to charity, I am giving a portion of them back. He has blessed me with time, so when I help another person, I am giving a portion of my time back to Him by helping them.

At times, I feel like the drummer boy, searching for what I can truly GIVE to God that isn't giving back. I have come to realize that there IS ONE THING that we have that doesn't come from God. It is something that we have to cultivate on our own. God helps us in cultivating it. But having this one gift rests more with us than it does with Him. That gift is HUMILITY.

There is only one gift I really have to give to Christ. It is the "broken and humbled heart God will not despise (Ps. 50:17)." Humility is a self-emptying proposition. It is humility that allows us to empty ourselves of anger and be filled with forgiveness towards someone else. It is humility that allows us to empty out pride and be filled with repentance towards Christ. It is humility that allows us to empty ourselves and be filled with Him.

If you think about it, no one can have any of the fruits of the Spirit without humility. Because in order to be loving, joyful, peaceful, patient, etc., you have empty yourself. You can't make it all about yourself and still have those things. In order to cultivate the fruits of the Spirit, one has to be filled with the Spirit. In order to be filled with the Spirit, one has to be rid of the things that spoil those fruits—hate, anger, impatience, etc. In order to have faith, the first step is the humble recognition that someone greater than me made me, and therefore I am not the center of the universe, that I should be revolving around God, not the other way around.

Humility makes it all about Him, and not about us. It's interesting to note that in the Old Testament, God sets the commandment of a ten percent tithe to the people of Israel. In the New Testament, God sets the commandment as turning over our whole life to Christ our God. It's supposed to be ALL about Him. To seek to continually decrease in ego, desire and power and to be filled instead with humility is the most profound act of faith there can be. St. Paul writes in Galatians 2:20: "I have been crucified with Christ; it is no longer I who live, but Christ who lives in me; and the life I now live in the flesh, I live by faith in the Son of God, who loved me and gave Himself for me." To live for Christ, to empty ourselves of our own desires and strive to follow after Him, this is humility. And it is humility that leads to glory. Remember the Parable of the Publican and the Pharisee, Jesus said "everyone who exalts himself will be humbled, but he who humbles himself will be exalted (Luke 18:14)."

Take a moment today and ponder on what gift you will bring to the manger this Christmas, realizing that there is really nothing material that you can bring. Take a moment and ponder on what kind of heart you will bring to the manger this year—one filled with pride? With pain? Or one filled with love, one filled with forgiveness, one filled with humility?

It is the broken and humbled heart that God wants as our gift this Christmas!

> Create in me a clean heart, O God, and put a new and right spirit within me. Cast me not away from Thy presence, and take not Thy Holy Spirit from me. Restore to me the joy of Thy salvation, and uphold me with a willing Spirit . . . O Lord, You shall open my lips, and my mouth

will declare Your praise. For if You desired sacrifice, I would give it; You will not be pleased with whole burnt offerings. A sacrifice to God is a broken spirit, a broken and humbled heart God will not despise. (Psalm 51, read at the Royal Hours of the Nativity)

Start wrapping your gift for Christ today!

December 23

The Meaning of the Word "Gratitude"

*Then opening their treasures, they offered Him **gifts**—gold, frankincense and myrrh. And being warned in a dream not to return to Herod, they departed to their own country by another way.*
—Matthew 2:11–12

In the Old Testament books of Exodus, Leviticus, Numbers, and Deuteronomy, one will find 613 commandments. Of these, there are the Ten Commandments, which most of us are familiar with. There are 603 others ones that we are not as familiar with. The Old Covenant between God and His people was based on these commandments.

In the New Testament, the Lord established a New Covenant, which summarized the Old Covenant with two commandments:

> You shall love the Lord your God with all your heart, and with all your soul, and with all your mind. This is the great and first commandment. And the second is like it, You shall love your neighbor as yourself. On these two commandments depend all the law and the prophets. (Matt. 22: 37–39)

And Jesus further condensed the two commandments into one word: LOVE.

He said to His disciples: "A new commandment I give to you, that you love one another; even as I have loved you, that you also love one another. By this all men will know that you are My disciples, if you have love for one another (John 13:34–35)."

So, our faith is built around a single word—LOVE.

In the next two days, you will have the opportunity to offer gifts. You will offer gifts to your family, your friends. And you will have the opportunity to offer a gift of yourself to Christ. How will you offer these gifts? Out of obligation? Or with love? Will you offer a gift out of love and after Christmas still hold a grudge with the person to whom you gave the gift? Offering a gift, whatever gift that may be, should always be done as a gesture of love. And if perfect love does not exist between you and the person you are giving to, or if it does not exist at this moment between you and the Lord, then the gift should be offered in a spirit of reconciliation, with an expressed desire to work towards a more perfect love.

In the next two days, you will also receive gifts from your family and friends. How will you receive them? Will it be with anger, or with gratitude? Of course, the answer is with gratitude, at least on the surface. No one is going to receive a gift and not offer at least a polite "thank you." The question is, how will we honor the giver? Will we receive with gratitude and still hold a grudge between us and them? Or will our gratitude reflect a spirit of reconciliation, with an expressed desire to work towards a better relationship? The offering of a gift, or the receiving of a gift is supposed to bring giver and receiver closer together. So, give with love, and receive with gratitude.

In the next two days, you will also receive a gift from Christ. Actually, there are many gifts we will receive from Christ. First, we will receive another Christmas, another year blessed with life that comes from the Giver of Life, the Lord. Second, most of us have someone to spend

Christmas with—family, friends—another gift from the Lord. Third, the food we eat, the laughter we'll have, the joy we'll feel, these are all gifts from the Lord. The most important gift of the Lord will be the opportunity to worship Him this Christmas—to pray in church, to sing hymns of praise to Him, to hear the scriptures once again, hopefully now with new ears and new hearts; and most importantly, to receive Him in the Eucharist, the Divine Thanksgiving.

When you receive Christ, through prayer, worship, or the Eucharist, how do you receive Him? With a sense of entitlement? With a sense of gratitude? Does this encounter between giver (Him) and receiver (you) bring you closer to Him? Or it is done out of mere habit? We are supposed to receive with gratitude, offering thanks to God with our words, and more important, with our actions. I have for a long time corrected those who use the phrase "take Communion" by saying that we "receive" Communion. We take things out of a sense of entitlement. We receive things with gratitude. So, receive Christ with gratitude, and after this holiday is over, keep gratitude as part of your daily life. We hear the phrase "Keep Christ in Christmas." But we need to keep Him in everyday life. And we need to thank Him not only on Christmas, but every day. We need to live for Him and in Him every day, not just on Christmas.

Gratitude is closely linked to optimism. The grateful person sees goodness and God in even the smallest of blessings. Undoubtedly, there will be many children who will be disappointed that they didn't get exactly what they asked for (especially if it is a very expensive gift). The grateful person finds joy and is thankful for even the smallest of gifts—another day, any expression of love, the smallest kindness. There are times in every life when we are disappointed with one another, and even times we get disappointed with God. This is where gratitude comes in—the grateful person sees opportunity and sees God in everything, even when things don't go as we wished or planned for them to go.

Will there be a gift that you will leave unopened under your tree? Of course not. We will open every gift, and open them eagerly. Don't leave the gift of Christ unopened this Christmas. Praise Him, thank Him, and worship Him. Receive Him in Holy Communion.

Many people are sad when they open the last gift. I wonder why. It's not like we have to wait until next Christmas to get another gift. We are receiving gifts all the time. Giving gifts should also be something that we do every day—and those gifts can be simple kindnesses, words of affirmation and encouragement, a sympathetic ear, and dozens of other examples that cost little in terms of time or money.

As we finish our gift wrapping, and in two days, our gift-giving and opening, remember this very important thing. It is not only on Christmas that we should offer gifts to one another. We should be offering gifts to someone EVERY day. It is not only on Christmas that we should offer our gifts to the Lord. We should offer Him something of ourselves every day. And it is not only on Christmas that we receive the Gift of Christ. There is at least one gift from Him to us EVERY day.

Give to Christ daily. Receive from Christ daily. Have gratitude towards Christ daily.

> What shall we offer you, O Christ, because You have appeared on earth as a man for our sakes? For each of the creatures made by You offers You its thanks: the Angels, their hymn; the heavens, the Star; the Shepherds, their wonder; the Magi, their gifts; the earth, the Cave; the desert the Manger; and we, a Virgin Mother. God before

the ages, have mercy on us. (Stichera from the Vespers of the Nativity. Trans. Fr. Seraphim Dedes)

Prepare to receive your gift from Christ. Prepare to offer your gifts to Him.

December 24

And the Word Became Flesh

And the Word became flesh and dwelt among us and we beheld His glory.
—John 1:14

For the past forty days we have been studying the Gospels of Matthew and Luke and their accounts of the Nativity. The Gospel of Mark makes no mention of the Nativity. It begins with the Baptism of Christ. The Gospel of John summarizes the Nativity in one verse: "And the Word became flesh and dwelt among us and we beheld His glory." In Nativity scenes and Christmas pageants, we are so enamored with the figures of the Nativity story—the angels, the shepherds, the Magi—that sometimes we forget the main figure in the story—our Lord Jesus Christ.

When we call the feast of Christmas "The birth of Jesus," this too causes confusion. My wife and I have been blessed with one child, who was born in a finite moment in time. Before his birth, we had no son. He did not exist. This is NOT true for Jesus Christ. St. John captures this best with the opening chapter of his Gospel:

> In the beginning was the Word, and the Word was with God, and the Word was God. He was in the beginning with God; all things were made through Him, and

without Him was not anything made that was made. (John 1:1–3)

As we examined in an earlier reflection, "Word of God" is another title given to the second person of the Trinity, who is also called Jesus, Christ, Son of God, Son of Man, Only-Begotten Son of the Father, Messiah, Savior.

It is easier to understand the beginning of John's Gospel if we insert *Christ* for *Word*, so please allow me to do this for better understanding: *In the Beginning was CHRIST, and CHRIST was with God, and Christ was (and is) God. Christ was in the beginning with God; all things were made through Christ* [He was co-Creator with God the Father and the Holy Spirit] *and without Christ was not anything made that was made.*

Continuing on with John's Gospel, *And Christ took on flesh and dwelt among us, and we beheld His Glory.*

The Feast of the Nativity is the day that the Son of God came to live among us. He took on flesh in the way that we do. He came into this world as a new-born baby. He didn't just drop in as an adult. And from the time of His Incarnation, He followed all the steps that we take. He grew up as we do. He learned to walk, He went to school, He had friends, He had struggles. The difference between us and Him is that throughout His life, He walked in tandem with God. He never ventured away from God, as we do when we sin. He came to show us the path to salvation. He came to show us how to live in God, with God, and for God. And He came to balance the equation, to die for our sins, to open a path back to Paradise for us.

So the Feast of the Nativity is not the BIRTH of Christ, but the Incarnation of the Son of God in the flesh. It is the day the Creator came to live with His Creation. It is the day that the uncontained God was "contained" in a human body.

The scriptural account of the Nativity that we have been studying for the past 40 days is captured in the Icon of the Nativity included in today's reflection. There are three distinct things that this icon depicts.

First, it captures the event of the Nativity. Mary gives birth to her first-born Son in a cave, because there is no room at any inn. Joseph is near-by, taking it all in.

Second, the icon captures that ALL of creation worshipped at the Nativity. All of Creation was present and invited to share in the miracle. The poor—the shepherds. The powerful—the Magi. The angels in heaven. The celestial bodies—the Star. The animals. The earth itself—the cave. All of Creation showed up to worship the Creator in its midst.

Third, the icon serves as an invitation to us to come and worship also. The manger is shown as a tomb, the swaddling bands are burial cloths. This IS the Creator, come to save us through the cross and the tomb. His purpose is clear. The cave is heaven—surrounded by jagged rocks, the cave itself is a setting of peace amidst a place of danger. We are called to follow, the way the Magi followed the star. We are all called—the call to the Shepherds is the call to everyone. Whatever your stage in life, whatever your status in society, all are welcomed. The heavens declare the glory of God. The angels sing God's praises and invite us to do the same.

When I study the icon of the Nativity, the figure of Joseph is who I relate to most of all. He sits at a distance. His thoughts are confused. He has been the loyal protector. He has put his reputation on the line. He has followed and trusted. And yet he is still trying to make sense of the whole thing. And that's okay. He's still there. He is still trying. It is a lesson to us to do the same.

Every person in the icon has followed a tough calling:

Mary has lost parents, given many years of her life in the temple, and has given birth to a Son whom she will see killed in a heinous manner.

Joseph has risked reputation to protect his betrothed who is with child that is not his. Joseph won't live long enough to see Jesus grow into a man.

The shepherds were the first to see the Christ, but still remained scorned outsiders. They weren't even important enough to be counted in the census, yet God counted them the first to be called to the manger.

The Magi left kingdoms and riches and followed the star. It was a two year journey in, and presumably a two year journey home. What possibly could have been left of their lives after a four year absence?

In their supreme sacrifice, in their trust, in their faith, all of these people received the greatest blessing. They beheld HIS GLORY. They beheld with their own eyes, the Son of God, made flesh, come to dwell among us. They were all profoundly changed for the experience. And all are profoundly honored both by God, and now by us.

Indeed, John captures the message of the feast in the most succinct way. We are called to behold His glory. This is the message of the Nativity. It is also the goal of every human life.

> Be not afraid.
> I bring you good news.
> Of a great joy.
> Which will come to all the world.
> For to you is born this day.
> A Savior, who is Christ the Lord. (Adapted from Luke 2: 10-11)

> Let us go, today.
> Rejoicing exceedingly with great joy.
> Opening our treasures. (Adapted from Matt 2: 10-11)

For the Word has become flesh.

Let us behold His Glory. (Adapted from John 1:14)

You righteous, be glad in heart; and the heavens, be exultant. Leap for joy, O mountains, at the birth of the Messiah. Resembling the Cherubim, the Virgin Maiden is seated and holds in her embraces God the Logos incarnate. The shepherds glorify the newborn Babe; Magi bring the Master their precious gifts. Angels are singing hymns of praise and say, "O Lord incomprehensible, glory to You."

The Father was well pleased; the Logos became flesh; and the Virgin gave birth to God who became man. A Star reveals Him; Magi bow in worship; Shepherds marvel, and creation rejoices. (The Praises, Orthros of the Nativity. Trans. Fr. Seraphim Dedes)

Have a Blessed Feast of the Nativity!

December 25

Read the Story

With our journey to the manger now complete, take a moment today and read the whole story again. Read it with someone else—your spouse, your parent, your child, your friend, your whole family. Sit around the table, or in front of your Christmas tree, and read the story, now hopefully understood with deeper meaning than ever before.

Now the birth of Jesus Christ took place in this way. When His mother Mary had been betrothed to Joseph, before they came together she was found to be with child of the Holy Spirit; and her husband Joseph, being a just man and unwilling to put her to shame, resolved to divorce her quietly. But as he considered this, behold, an angel of the Lord appeared to him in a dream, saying, "Joseph, son of David, do not fear to take Mary your wife, for that which is conceived in her is of the Holy Spirit; she will bear a Son, and you shall call His name Jesus, for he will save His people from their sins." All this took place to fulfill what the Lord had spoken by the prophet:

> "Behold, a virgin shall conceive and bear a Son,
> and His name shall be called Emmanuel"
> (which means "God with us").

When Joseph woke from sleep, he did as the angel of the Lord commanded him; he took his wife, but knew her not until she had borne a Son; and he called His name Jesus. (Matt. 1:18–25)

In those days a decree went out from Caesar Augustus that all the world should be enrolled. This was the first enrollment, when Quirinius was governor of Syria. And all went to be enrolled, each to his own city. And Joseph also went up from Galilee, from the city of Nazareth, to Judea, to the city of David, which is called Bethlehem, because he was of the house and lineage of David, to be enrolled with Mary, his betrothed, who was with child. And while they were there, the time came for her to be delivered. And she gave birth to her first-born Son and wrapped Him in swaddling clothes, and laid Him in a manger, because there was no place for them in the inn. And in that region there were shepherds out in the field, keeping watch over their flocks by night. And an angel of the Lord appeared to them, and the glory of the Lord shone around them, and they were filled with fear. And the angel said to them, "Be not afraid; for behold, I bring you good news of a great joy which will come to all the people; for to you is born this day in the city of David a Savior, who is Christ the Lord. And this will be a sign for you: you will find a Babe wrapped in swaddling clothes and lying in a manger." And suddenly there was with the angel a multitude of the heavenly host praising God and saying, "Glory to God in the highest, and on earth peace among men with whom He is pleased!" When the angels went away from them into heaven, the shepherds said to one another, "Let us go over to Bethlehem and see this thing that has happened, which the Lord has made known to us." And they went with haste, and found Mary and Joseph, and the Babe lying in a manger. And when they saw it they made known the saying which had been told them concerning this Child; and all who heard it wondered at what the shepherds told them. But Mary kept all these things, pondering them in her heart. And the shepherds returned, glorifying and praising God for all they had heard and seen, as it had been told them. (Luke 2:1–20)

Now when Jesus was born in Bethlehem of Judea in the days of Herod the king, behold, wise men from the East came to Jerusalem, saying, "Where is He who has been born King of the Jews? For we have seen His star in the East, and have come to worship Him." When Herod the king heard this, he was troubled, and all Jerusalem with him; and assembling all the chief Priests and scribes of the people, he inquired of them where the Christ was to be born. They told him, "In Bethlehem of Judea; for so it is written by the prophet:

'And you, O Bethlehem, in the land of Judah, are
by no means least among the rulers of Judah; for
from you shall come a ruler who will govern my
people Israel.'"

Then Herod summoned the wise men secretly and ascertained from them what time the star appeared; and he sent them to Bethlehem, saying, "Go and search diligently for the Child, and when you have found him bring me word, that I too may come and worship Him." When they had heard the king they went their way; and lo, the star which they had seen in the East went before them, till it came to rest over the place where the Child was. When they saw the star, they rejoiced exceedingly with great joy; and going into the house they saw the Child with Mary His mother, and they fell down and worshiped Him. Then, opening their treasures, they offered Him gifts, gold and frankincense and myrrh. And being warned in a dream not to return to Herod, they departed to their own country by another way. (Matt. 2:1–12)

Your Nativity, O Christ our God, has caused the light of knowledge to rise upon the world. For therein the worshippers of the stars were by a star instructed to worship You, the Son of Righteousness, and to know You as Orient from on high. Glory to You, O Lord. (Apolytikion of the Nativity. Trans. Fr. Seraphim Dedes)

On this day the Virgin gives birth unto the Super-essential. To the Unapproachable, earth is providing the grotto. Angels sing and with the shepherds offer up glory. Following a star the Magi are still proceeding. He was born for our salvation, a newborn Child, the pre-eternal God. (Kontakion of the Nativity. Trans. Fr. Seraphim Dedes)

Christ is Born! Glorify Him!

December 26

He Understands Us

*Therefore **He had to be made like His brethren in every respect,** so that He might become a merciful and faithful high priest in the service of God, to make expiation for the sins of the people. For because He Himself has suffered and been tempted, He is able to help those who are tempted.*
—Hebrews 2:14–18 (Epistle Reading on December 26)

Christ is Born! Glorify Him! (This is the Orthodox greeting from December 25-January 5)

In the Orthodox world we celebrate the Nativity from December 25–31, then the feast of the Circumcision of Christ/St. Basil on January 1, the forefeast of Epiphany from January 2–5, and Epiphany from January 6–14. Having marked a forty-day period of Advent, we go into "feast" mode for the next few weeks. In fact, there is no fasting from December 25 through January 4.

In order to balance the equation (see reflection of November 27), Jesus Christ had to experience all of the things that the human being experiences. And in order to do that, He had to become a human being. Though conceived by the Holy Spirit and the Virgin Mary, He was "born" as we are. He fulfilled the conditions of the Law when He was presented in the Temple on His fortieth day (which our church commemorates on February 2, and which you can read about in Luke 2:22:38). He went to the temple like other boys His age and learned the scriptures. At age twelve, when His parents went to Jerusalem, (Luke 2: 41–52) He was in the temple with Jewish scholars and temple leaders, reciting verses of scripture.

Because He was made like us, He understands us. As St. Paul writes in his letter to the Hebrews, "because He Himself has suffered and been tempted, He is able to help those who are tempted." God knows all things, but since the Son of God has walked this earth as one of us, He understands what it is like to be one of us. The Bible tells us that in His earthly life, Jesus felt many of the same things that we feel. He even understands temptation and the assaults of the Devil. In Matthew 4:1–11, we read an account of the Temptations of Christ, where Christ was in the desert for forty days where He was fasting and preparing for His ministry and at the same time was constantly tempted and tormented by the Devil. Certainly there must have been other temptations. Righteous anger at the money-changers in the temple (John 2: 13–22) could have gone too far but it didn't. We know that Christ was in agony in the Garden of Gethsemane (Matthew 26:39) as He prayed for the cup of suffering to go away if it was His Father's will. There were very human emotions of fear, sadness, perhaps even teetering on doubt. There is no doubt that Christ understood the human condition that we all suffered from. Because not only did He suffer a human death, but He suffered from the same conditions we suffer from throughout His earthly life.

But there was a greater reason that Christ came to be with us. Not only did He come to understand us, but He came for us to understand what it is like to be one with Him, to be one with God. He came to save us from our human condition and show us the path to Godliness. Through His ministry, teachings and miracles, He showed us what it means to have love, compassion and mercy. Through His death, He showed us what it means to have faith and total trust in God. Through His Resurrection, He showed us the path to everlasting life. If we live in Christ, and if we die with faith in Christ, then we will also be Resurrected with Christ. St. Paul writes in his letter to the Romans, "For if we have been united with Him in a death like His, we shall certainly be united with Him in a Resurrection like His (Rom. 6:5)."

The BEST explanation of the Nativity, perhaps, comes from one of the church fathers, St. Athanasios, who lived in the fourth century and was one of the bishops at the First Ecumenical Council in Nicea in 325 A.D. when the Creed was written. He wrote a treatise entitled *On the Incarnation*. In the treatise, he wrote:

> The Word was made flesh in order that we might be made
> gods . . . Just as the Lord, putting on the body, became a
> man, so also we men are both deified through His flesh,
> and henceforth inherit everlasting life . . . For the Son of
> God became man so that we might become God.

Christ did not come only to save us from our sins, but to raise us up in glory with Him, to deify *us*, so that we can live eternally with Christ, in union with Christ, in a state of Paradise, like Christ.

Many people will be making a trip back to the store today to return Christmas presents that were not wanted, or that just didn't fit right. Make sure that the gift of Christ is something you hold onto and treasure. It's something everyone wants and needs, and something that fits everyone *just right*!

> He whom nothing can contain has been contained in
> a womb. He is in the Father's bosom and His Mother's

177

embrace. How can this be, but as He knows and willed and was well pleased. Fleshless as He was, He willingly took flesh. And He Who Is became what He was not, for us. And while departing not from His own nature, He shared in our nature's substance. So Christ was born with dual natures, wishing to replenish the world on high. (Kathisma from the Orthros of the Nativity. Trans. Fr. Seraphim Dedes)

Strive to be like Christ today!

December 27

We Are His Children

*But when the time had fully come, God sent forth His Son, born of woman, born under the law, to redeem those who were under the law, so that we might receive adoption as sons. And because **you are sons,** God has sent the Spirit of His Son into our hearts, crying "Abba! Father!" So through God you are no longer a slave but a son, and if a son, then an heir.*
—Galatians 4:4–6 (Epistle Reading from Christmas)

*C*hrist is Born! Glorify Him!

Many of us remember the musical *Annie*. It was about a little orphan girl who lived "a hard-knock life" in a dingy orphanage with a house mother, Miss Hannigan, who treated her terribly. Annie tried to escape to find her parents but was caught and returned to the orphanage. Later on, a billionaire businessman, Oliver Warbucks (Daddy Warbucks) invited Annie to come to his mansion for the Christmas holidays. He put out a reward for anyone who could prove that they were Annie's real parents. Meanwhile, he really began to love Annie. Some deceit led to him almost losing Annie but eventually he adopted her. She left the former life that she had, and found a safe haven with a new father. She reaped not only material sufficiency, but emotional stability.

In many ways, before Christ came, the human race was like Little Orphan Annie. It had not been abandoned by its Father, for God had never abandoned His children, but rather people had estranged themselves from God. Christ came to show us a better way. He chose us, He chose all of us, and wants to rescue us from the dangers of those who have no "parent" to guide them. And He wants us to come to His house, where the blessings are overwhelming. He does not want us only to feel like guests though. He wants to adopt us as His children, with all the benefits of "sonship," including a hefty inheritance, which is eternal life.

There is a difference between being a son and being a servant. We are servants of God, but we are also His children. A servant is hired. A son is chosen. A servant can be fired. A son is for life. God doesn't desire to have us sit at His table as servants. He wants us to sit as His children. God has shown us the way to Him is by serving one another, and by serving one another we serve Him. When Jesus sat at the table with His disciples at the Last Supper, He washed THEIR feet, showing them what it means to be a servant. By dying on the cross for us, He has shown the kind of love that only a parent can show—He gave His life for His children.

When we are estranged from God, we are like the Little Orphan Annie, living without proper spiritual and emotional support. Eventually we will all suffer from lack of material things—think about the person on their death bed who is materially rich but still confined to the hospital bed. God wants us to have emotional and spiritual riches. The emotionally rich are filled with love—love for others, knowing that others love them. And the spiritually rich are also filled with love—because they love God and they KNOW that God loves them, and not as servants, but as children. The spiritually rich are waiting for their turn to go to the "mansion" of their "Daddy." Emotional riches are acquired by learning to love your neighbor and by serving your neighbor with a servant's heart. Spiritual riches come from loving God and recognizing that you are a child of God, who loves God as a Father, who trusts God as a child trusts his father.

One crucially important difference between our earthly fathers and our Heavenly Father—in order for us to be inheritors of our earthly fathers, they have to die, and this makes us rightfully sad. Christ has already died for us, and lives again. The inheritance is already ours to be had. He doesn't have to die for us to have our inheritance because that has already happened. And even though we won't receive the full measure of our inheritance until we die, we receive pieces of our inheritance everyday through the blessings He bestows on us in this life, in preparation for everlasting life.

Being a Christian doesn't necessarily spare you from a hard-knock life in this world, but it opens the door for you to be an heir of everlasting blessings in the world to come.

> Your Kingdom, O Christ God, is a kingdom of all the ages, and Your dominion is from generation to generation. You who were incarnate by the Holy Spirit and became man by the ever-Virgin Mary, have shone on us as light, by Your advent, O Christ God. Light of light, the brightness of the Father, you have brightened all creation. Everything that breathes praises You, the express image of the Father's glory. O God, the One who is and who pre-existed, and who shone forth from the Virgin, have mercy on us. (Stichera from Vespers of the Nativity. Trans. Fr. Seraphim Dedes)

Honor our Father today!

December 28

We Have to Take the Same Journey

Now when the magi had departed, behold an angel of the Lord appeared to Joseph in a dream and said, "Rise, take the child and His mother and flee to Egypt, and remain there till I tell you; for Herod is about to search for the child, to destroy Him." And he rose and took the child and his mother by night, and departed to Egypt, and remained there until the death of Herod. This was to fulfill what the Lord had spoken by the prophet,
"Out of Egypt have I called my Son."
—Matthew 2:13–15 (Gospel Reading, Sunday after Christmas)

*C*hrist is born! Glorify Him!

One of the many titles given to Jesus Christ is "the second Adam." Christ comes and fulfills what the first Adam could not do. The first Adam lived in Paradise. By "restoring" the fallen image of Adam, Christ shows us the gateway back to the Paradise enjoyed by Adam. In His earthly ministry, Christ retraced all the steps of the Old Testament. Not only did He fulfill the prophecies of the Old Testament (more on that is coming in the next few reflections), but He took the journey of the Israelites to Egypt and then back out of Egypt.

For those who don't remember, the Israelites went to Egypt to escape a famine in their land that would have brought certain death. After staying as sojourners in a strange land, where they eventually became enslaved, they were liberated and once again went back to the land of Canaan, their original homeland.

Christ follows the same journey—under the threat of death by King Herod, He escaped to Egypt, where He remained, a stranger in a strange land, until Herod had died and it was safe to return to His homeland.

Trusting God in our life journeys is again a theme today. First, the Magi, who had trusted in a star that they followed for two years, believing it would lead to the Christ, again had to trust in God. "Being warned in a dream not to return to Herod and departing to their own country by another way (Matt. 2:12)," they bypassed Herod's palace on the way out of town. Think of the consequences that could have had. Herod was furious and would kill all the male children in Bethlehem because of that, though he very easily could have ordered the death of the Magi as well.

And Mary and Joseph had to take another leap of faith when they were told by the Angel to go to Egypt until further notice. For their journey to Bethlehem, they only had the possessions they could carry with them. Joseph most likely thought he'd return to Nazareth, to his home and his business, after the quick trip to Bethlehem for the census. Now, there was no opportunity to go home, his meager belongings would have to suffice for this journey. How would he provide an income? What would happen to his carpentry business after a long absence from home? And yet Joseph and Mary too the journey to Egypt, strangers again in a strange land, and God provided for them because they trusted in Him. We are not told how, only that they safely made it to Egypt, safely lived there, and eventually safely returned to Nazareth.

Our life journeys also have strange and unforeseen twists and turns in them. Many times God asks us to take a detour, and sometimes another detour on that. Many times we have to really dig deep and trust in God, for sometimes what He asks of us is daunting. Some of life's journeys can be downright scary.

I'm sure if you think about it, we've all had the experience of the flight to Egypt, being strangers in a strange land—that might be when you went to college, or relocated to a new town, or started a new job. We all have to take some leap of faith. When we do it with God, and more important, when we do it for God, we always arrive at a "safe" ending, even though the passage itself might be filled with danger. And most important, even though the ending might not be the place where we thought He would lead us. This is very important—sometimes the end of the journey is not where we would have wanted it to be. But if we stay faithful to God, and follow the journey to where HE wants it to end, we will find ultimate safety with Him.

Christ took the journey of the Israelites from Egypt to the Promised Land. We too must pass through our own "Egypt" on our way to the Promised Land.

> Working signs of old the Master saved the people, replacing fluid waves of the sea with dry land. Now born of a Maid by His own will, He has made passable a way to heaven. Him, in essence equal to mankind and the Father, we glorify. (Iambic Katavasias of the Nativity. Trans. Fr. Seraphim Dedes)

Trust God!

December 29

Rachel Is Still Weeping for Her Children

Then Herod, when he saw that he had been tricked by the wise men, was in a furious rage, and he sent and killed all the male children in Bethlehem and in all that region who were two years old or under, according to the time which he had ascertained from the wise men. Then was fulfilled what was spoken by the prophet Jeremiah: "A voice was heard in Ramah, wailing and loud lamentation, **Rachel weeping for her children**; *she refused to be consoled because they were no more."*
—Matthew 2:16–18 (Gospel Reading, Sunday after Christmas)

Christ is born! Glorify Him!

In this joy of this season, in the glory of this story of Christ's Nativity, there is one dark chapter that must be mentioned, which is the slaughter of the innocents by King Herod. When I read this Gospel passage each year during the Divine Liturgy on the Sunday after the Nativity, I always get tears in my eyes as I read the phrase "Rachel weeping for her children." I think of the sadness in the world, of mothers and fathers who don't have their children at Christmas because they have succumbed to disease, accident, war, terrorism, or any other factor that causes premature death. I also think of people who are like King Herod—people who wish to harm the message of Christianity and those who adhere to it. Indeed, in many corners of the world, "Rachel is still weeping for her children."

Please take a moment today to thank God for His blessings. Pray for those who are weeping today for whatever reason. I'm sure there are some you know, and many more that you don't. Many of these reflections include some call to action. Today's call is for all of us to be a little more attentive—make sure you know the person who works next to you in the office, or who lives next door, or who sits next to you in the pews on Sunday. Part of loving our neighbor means comforting our neighbor, and in order to do that, we have to know our neighbor, so we know who needs a shoulder to cry on. We all have to work at creating environments which let our neighbors know that we are ready and willing to do that.

In John 1: 4–5, we read "In Him (the Word) was life, and the life was the light of men. The light shines in the darkness, and the darkness has not overcome it." Only the Light of Christ, and the hope found in Him, can dry the tears of Rachel and soften the heart of Herod. "Let your Light so shine before men (Matt. 5:16)," so that you can be a help to those who need help, in whatever way help is needed.

> Since the Lord Jesus was born of the holy Virgin, the universe has been illumined. Shepherds were keeping watch, and Magi were adoring Him, and Angels were singing praises, and Herod was troubled; for God appeared in the flesh, yes, the Savior of our souls. (Stichera from Vespers of the Nativity. Trans. Fr. Seraphim Dedes)

Give an extra hug to someone today!

December 30

Promises Kept

*But when Herod died, behold, an angel of the Lord appeared in a dream
to Joseph in Egypt, saying, "Rise, take the Child and His mother, and
go to the land of Israel, for those who sought the Child's life are dead."
And he rose and took the Child and His mother, and went to the land of
Israel. But when he heard that Archelaus reigned over Judea in place of
his father Herod, he was afraid to go there, and being warned in a dream
he withdrew to the district of Galilee. And he went and dwelt in a city
called Nazareth, that **what was spoken by the prophets might be
fulfilled,** "He shall be called a Nazarene."*
—Matthew 2:19–23 (Gospel Reading, Sunday after Christmas)

*C*hrist is Born! Glorify Him!

There are hundreds of prophecies in the Old Testament that are
fulfilled in the New Testament. In these series of reflections we have
already encountered several:

> Behold a Virgin shall conceive and bear a Son and His
> name shall be called "Emmanuel." (Matt. 1:23; originally
> stated in Isa. 7:14.)

And you, O Bethlehem, in the land of Judah, are by no means least among the rulers of Judah; for from you shall come a ruler who will govern my people Israel. *(*Matt. 2:6; originally stated in Mic. 5:2)

Out of Egypt have I called my Son. (Matt. 2:15; originally stated in Hosea 11:1)

A voice was heard in Ramah, wailing and loud lamentation, Rachel weeping for her children, she refused to be consoled for they were no more. *(*Matt. 2:18; originally stated in Jer. 31:15)

He shall be called a Nazarene. *(*Matt. 2:23; alluded to in Judg. 13:3 and Isa. 11:1)

For hundreds of years, and in hundreds of places in the Scriptures, prophecies were written about a coming Messiah. When Christ came to earth at the Nativity, and in His ministry that followed, these prophecies began to be fulfilled in rapid succession. There are literally hundreds of prophecies in the Old Testament, and all of them were fulfilled in a single person: Jesus Christ. This provides irrefutable evidence that this man is the Christ. How could all these things happen to one person and He not be the Christ?

St. Matthew wrote his Gospel primarily to a Jewish audience. St. Luke wrote primarily to Gentiles. St. Matthew in his Gospel, made the most references to the prophecies, as a way of telling the people, "See, this is the person that has been prophesied about for hundreds of years and ALL of these prophecies are being fulfilled in HIM!!!"

So begins almost a domino effect. The dominos, so to speak, are set up in the Old Testament prophecies, and Jesus Christ begins to knock them down one at a time so that as His work began, people would begin to see in Him the signs that they had heard about for centuries. When His work was finished, there would be no doubt that this is the Christ, the Son of God, the promised Messiah.

There are still some skeptics who wonder if it is all true. There is an historical record, in addition to the prophecies being fulfilled, which supports the ministry of Christ. The slaughter of the innocents is an historical event. It happened in about 4 B.C. when there was a King Herod, who died shortly thereafter. The crucifixion took place on the 13th day of the Jewish month of Nisan, in what we now call 29 A.D. There was a person named Jesus who was preaching, teaching, and healing—this is historical record as well. The matter of faith is did this person Jesus Christ, who was crucified and buried, rise from the dead? This is where historians disagree. The Bible says that Jesus was seen risen from the dead by over 500 people (I Cor. 15:6). The sheer amount of evidence in prophecies fulfilled in the person of Jesus Christ—hundreds of prophecies fulfilled in ONE person— leaves no doubt that this person the world saw as Jesus *is* the Christ.

The prophecies are important because they set the stage for what was to come. They give us a checklist, so to speak, to verify that Jesus is the Christ. Jesus, in His words that are told in the Gospels, also made a number of promises to us, especially about the Kingdom of God. And just as the prophecies of the Old Testament came true in Christ, His prophecies and parables about the Kingdom of Heaven will come true for us. It takes faith to believe and to wait. The New Testament is all about promises of the Old Testament being fulfilled. And everlasting life will be all about the teachings of Christ being fulfilled to the faithful forever.

Jonah, as he sat in the sea's deepest caverns, implored to come to You and out of the tempest. But as for me, by the tyrant's arrows wounded, I pray to You, O Christ, the Destroyer of evil, come to me quicker than my soul's own indifference. (Iambic Katavasias of the Nativity. Trans. Fr. Seraphim Dedes)

Stay faithful today!

December 31

Tell Me How it Really Is

*And **at the end of eight days**, when He was circumcised, **He was called**
Jesus, the name given by the angel before He was conceived in the womb.*
—Luke 2:21 (Gospel Reading, January 1)

Christ is Born! Glorify Him!
A story is told of a woman who prepared a ham for her family to eat every year on New Year's Day. When she prepared the ham, she cut a large piece off one end and placed it at the side of the larger portion of the ham in her cooking pan. Her daughter watched her mother for years prepare the ham for New Year's. When she had a home and family of her own, the daughter also followed the "tradition" of making a ham for New Year's Day. She, too, like her mother, would cut one end of the ham off and place it beside the rest of the ham in her cooking pan. One day, her daughter asked her, "mommy, why do you cut the end of the ham off and place it next to the bigger portion in the pan?" She answered, "well, this is the way that Yiayia (Greek for grandmother) does it. I'm not really sure why I do it, let's go ask her." So, they went to Yiayia's house and asked her. Yiayia got out her pan. She said to her daughter and granddaughter, "You see this pan, it is very small. The ham does not fit. So I cut the end off of the ham and put it to the side." The daughter felt a little perplexed at the moment. Here she thought that the cutting off of the end of the ham was

an integral part of the New Year's ritual. And now she realized that this wasn't part of the feast at all—it was unnecessary to cut the ham in two pieces because she had a large pan to cook it in.

This is how traditions are born. Something we just do and have really no idea why we are doing it. There are some Traditions (with a capital T) in the Church that are born directly from scripture. There are other traditions (with a small t) that come from our Yiayias; we call these old wives tales or in the Greek culture *yiayialogy*, and because "yiayia is never wrong," these traditions grow into really incorrect understanding and sometimes incorrect practice in the Church.

There is a Greek tradition where a child is not named until it is baptized. There is no scriptural basis for this whatsoever. The scriptures say very clearly that Jesus was circumcised when He was eight days old, according to Jewish Law, and was given the name Jesus at that time. There is a prayer in the Orthodox Church for a child who is eight days old, where the child receives its name and receives it from its parents, not its godparents, another cultural custom. All of our Traditions are based in scripture. This one is no exception. Jesus was not baptized until He was thirty. Certainly He would have been called a name before that!

There are some other important things to note about the circumcision of Christ, which is commemorated on the 8th day after His Nativity. It was the law that anyone who was one of God's people, a Jewish male, needed to be circumcised. They needed a mark on them to mark them as a child of God. So, Jesus followed the Law. He did not come to abolish the law, but to supersede the Law. In order to supersede the Law, He needed to first do the things that the Law required, one of which was being circumcised.

In modern Christianity, a mark of God is still required among God's children. No, the mark is not circumcision of the flesh (the decision to circumcise a child is a medical decision, made in consultation with a doctor—there is no religious requirement to circumcise a child), but rather a circumcision of the heart. In Romans 2:28–29, St. Paul writes:

> For he is not a real Jew who is one outwardly, nor is true circumcision something external and physical. He is a Jew who is one inwardly, and real circumcision is a matter of the heart, spiritual and not literal.

The sign of the *circumcision of the heart* is baptism, the mark of God upon each of us, an indelible mark of God upon our hearts. There is still a ritual that we undergo in order to become a Christian, and that ritual is baptism. The idea of undergoing a ritual entrance into the faith is a Tradition from the Old Testament. Jesus underwent the ritual of circumcision, and afterwards, inaugurated a new ritual we now know as Baptism.

The point of today's reflection is to say that reading scripture is really important. It is really important to understand what we believe and where our beliefs come from. Many times our cultural ideas are not necessarily in line with what scripture says, hence the eight-day naming versus naming at a baptism. It is also important to mention that we worship neither *Tradition* nor *tradition*. We don't worship scripture either. We worship Christ. Scripture is the basis of correct Traditions. Traditions (large T) help us have a framework in which to practice our faith; traditions (small t) needlessly confuse us and in some ways inhibit us from learning and practicing the faith correctly. As you make your New Year's resolutions today to put into practice tomorrow, make reading scripture, even small amounts, part of your daily life.

> In essence being God, most compassionate Master, You assumed human nature without transmutation. Fulfilling

the Law of Your own will You accepted circumcision in the flesh, to bring an end to the shadow and to remove the passions that cover us. Glory to Your benevolence o Lord; glory to Your compassion; glory to Your inexpressible condescension o Word. (Apolytikion of January 1. Trans. by Fr. Seraphim Dedes)

Read the Scriptures today!

January 1

Happy New Year's Resolutions

*And He went down with them and came to Nazareth, and was **obedient**
to them; and His mother kept **all these things in her heart**. And Jesus
increased in wisdom and in stature, and in favor with God and man.*
—Luke 2:51–52 (Gospel Reading, January 1)

*C*hrist is born! Glorify Him!

Today, by God's grace, we enter into a new year. I often thank
God that He has fixed the day at 24 hours and the year at 365 days, that
we constantly have opportunities to make new beginnings provided for
us and we don't even need to go and seek them out. Today marks a new
year. It is a day that we greet with joy—we've lived to see another year. It
is a year that we should greet with optimism—whatever happened last
year is over, we all start with a clean slate. At 12:01, no one had had a bad
moment in 2016 yet. And we begin the year, many of us, with resolve.
We make resolutions to do new things, or to do things we've done but do
them more consistently.

Most resolutions fade in short order. Plans for strict dieting or rig-
orous exercise, to the person who has never done either, usually do not last
long. That's why whatever resolution you make should be something small
and manageable. You can always resolve to do MORE later on.

On your list of New Year's Resolutions should be some spiritual resolutions. While everyone will have some different spiritual resolutions based on where you are in your Christian life, you should model your resolutions around today's scripture verse.

Obedience-Without order, there is chaos. That is true in households, in businesses, in society and in spirituality. There has to be some order to our spiritual life and the order is found in the commandments of God, and in being obedient to them. Today's verse is from the Gospel passage about Jesus visiting the temple at age twelve. He visited Jerusalem with His parents and after His parents had left, He stayed behind in the temple. He had His own idea to be with the temple teachers. This disappointed His parents and the Gospel says that Jesus changed course, returned to Nazareth and was obedient to His parents. In the New Year, resolve to be more obedient to the commandments of God, even when they don't match with your own interests and ideas.

Keep the things of God in your heart—We keep important things and important people close to our hearts. We think often about the people who are important to us. We have sports allegiances, mottos and other things at the forefront of our minds and hearts. Keep the things of God front and center in your mind and heart. You do this by checking in with God on a daily basis—talk to Him through prayer, listen to Him through scripture. It doesn't have to be a lengthy session. A few minutes is all it takes to keep the things of God in the forefront of your heart. If you are only checking in once a week at church, it is much harder to keep God in the forefront. It's like He's on the front burner on Sundays and on a back burner the rest of the week. Make sure He occupies your front burner at least for a few moments each day through prayer and scripture reading.

Increase in wisdom and stature—Everyone should have a goal to be better at whatever they are doing by the end of 2016. I hope at the end of 2016, I am a better husband, a better father, a better priest, a better friend, a better Christian than I am as we begin the year. We should always strive to be better in our lives. Better does not mean quantitative increase, but qualitative increase. Better does not necessarily mean I need to earn a better salary or drive a better car. The *better* we are shooting for should be for improvement in positions we hold—to do a better job at the things we do, not necessarily to reap a bigger financial reward.

And in favor with God and man—If you have a goal to be a better Christian in 2016, the easiest places to start are working on your relationships with God and your fellow man. If we want to increase in favor with God, we can do that by resolving to spend more time with God. For those who do not pray regularly, start off with a couple of minutes every day dedicated to prayer. If you are already praying regularly, read a page or two of scripture each day. For those who are already doing both, consider reading a few pages of a theology book or a spiritually uplifting book each day. For those who do not worship regularly, make it a goal to get to church each Sunday. For those who are already doing this, try to add one additional weekday service every month of two. Make a small incremental change this New Year and make is a permanent change.

As for finding greater favor with *man*, this comes through additional gestures of love and concern toward your fellow man. One worthwhile resolution is to try to do one act of unexpected kindness every day. I remember from my years as a Boy Scout, our slogan was "Do a good turn daily." Make a conscious effort to do one unexpected act of kindness each day.

Visit us with Your goodness, Lord; manifest Yourself to us through Your rich compassion. Grant us seasonable weather and fruitful seasons; send gentle showers upon the earth so that it may bear fruit; bless the crown of the year of Your goodness. Prevent schism in the Church; pacify the raging of the heathen. Quickly stop the uprisings of heresies by the power of Your Holy Spirit. Receive us all into Your Kingdom. Declare us to be sons and daughters of the light and of the day. Grant us Your peace and love, Lord our God, for You have given all things to us. (From the Liturgy of St. Basil. Trans. by Holy Cross Greek Orthodox Seminary Press)

Have a great first day of the New Year!

January 2

A Worthy Epitaph for a Life Well Lived

As for you, always be steady, endure suffering, do the work of an evangelist, fulfill your ministry. For I am already on the point of being sacrificed, the time of my departure has come. **I have fought the good fight, I have finished the race, I have kept the faith.** *Henceforth there is laid up for me the crown of righteousness, which the Lord, the righteous judge, will award to me on that Day, and not only to me but also to all who have loved His appearing.*
—Second Timothy 4:5–8 (Epistle on Sunday before Epiphany)

*C*hrist is born! Glorify Him!

Have you ever thought of what you might want as your epitaph, what you'd want people to say about you when your earthly life is over? I remember having to do an assignment like this in school a couple of times, where we had to write something for our tombstone and something for our obituary. It was designed to get us thinking not only how we want to be remembered, but are we living a life that will have people remembering us as we hoped they would. I think about this once in a while, and as we begin a new year, it is a good time to think about it again. More important, however, than what people think about me, is what does God think about me? And do my hopes for God's thoughts about me match what I am currently doing in my life.

On the Sunday before Epiphany, the Epistle Lesson is always taken from II Timothy 4:5–8. This passage includes the best epitaph you could write for a Christian: "I have fought the good fight, I have finished the race, I have kept the faith." As we begin a new year, as we seek to grow closer to Christ in this new year, reflect on this verse.

The entire passage is framed around this verse. If you want to fight a good fight, then you have to be steady. Every life experiences its share of suffering. But we also know that it is suffering that produces character. St. Paul writes in his Epistle to the Romans that "we rejoice in our sufferings, knowing that suffering produces endurance, and endurance produces character and character produces hope, and hope does not disappoint us, because God's love has been poured into our hearts through the Holy Spirit which has been given to us (Rom. 5:3–5)." No year passes without something good happening. And likewise, no year passes without some trial or tribulation. The *good fight* is one that is fought with consistency. We do not need to be a super-Christian, just a steady one. And we do not want to go through periods of spiritual ecstasy followed by spiritual mediocrity. Better to keep a steady pace, for the race is a marathon, not a sprint.

Part of the race is to be an evangelist, to witness for Christ in some way. The easiest way is to love your neighbor. Even if the name of Christ is not mentioned, most of the time a quiet example is more effective than a vocal teaching. But there will be times this year, there will be conversations, where you will think about Christ, where you will think, "should I offer to pray here?" and then you will make a choice. We will all experience this. We will all have occasions to bring Christ or prayer into a conversation and it will come up naturally. What will you do at that moment? Go for what you are supposed to do? Or be frightened and timid about mentioning the name of the Lord?

Marathon runners do not think of the entire race at one time. They think about the race in increments, in miles, in markers. They focus on running one mile at a time, they focus on the pace of a single mile, not the pace of the entire race. The race is won by running each individual mile well. Put the miles together and you have a well-run race. This year, we will run a segment of our life race. Some us of are running the first mile or two (if you are young or a new Christian); others are somewhere in the middle and some are close to the end. Focus on running YOUR mile well. Focus on the mile ahead of you. For those who have not run well to this point, it doesn't do much good to look back and lament. Look forward and focus on running the next mile well. The good news with God is that He doesn't expect anyone to WIN the race, only to FINISH the race. St. Paul didn't write, "I have won the race," or "I have put my opponents to shame." He wrote, "I have finished the race."

And how does God want us to cross the finish line? He wants us to have kept the faith. There are many times when I minister to people who are at the end of life. They may be very sick, very tired. They may have had wonderful successes which have been forgotten because they lived twenty years past their retirement. And I will encourage them to "keep the faith." What good does it do the marathon runner to lead the entire race and then stop in the last mile? I'm reminded of watching the Indy 500 one year where one driver was out in front by a comfortable margin and inexplicably crashed into the wall with one turn to go. The announcers had all but declared him the winner, and then he didn't win. I've seen other races where the driver ran out of gas with only a few hundred yards to go and went from winner to not finishing. Again, we don't need to win anything—we are in competition with no one. We need to finish the race, and we need to keep the faith while finishing the race. God promises a reward, a crown of righteousness, to those who finish.

As we begin a new year, focus on running a steady race each day. Don't let hardships ruin your steady pace. And don't let disappointments threaten your faith. Fight a good fight, run today's segment of the race (string days and years together and then finish, but focus on running today's segment today) and keep (and grow) in the faith.

> Our God, the God who saves, You teach us justly to thank You for the good things which You have done and still do for us. You are our God who has accepted these Gifts. Cleanse us from every defilement of flesh and spirit, and teach us how to live in holiness by Your fear, so that receiving the portion of Your Holy Gifts with a clear conscience we may be united with the Holy Body and Blood of Your Christ. Having received them worthily, may we have Christ dwelling in our hearts, and may we become the temple of Your Holy Spirit. Yes, our God, let none of us be guilty before these, Your awesome and heavenly Mysteries, nor be infirm in body and soul by partaking of them unworthily. But enable us, even up to our last breath, to receive a portion of Your Holy Gifts worthily, as provision for eternal life and as an acceptable defense at the awesome judgment seat of Your Christ. So that we also, together with all the saints who throughout the ages have pleased You, may become partakers of Your eternal good things, which You, Lord, have prepared for those who love You. (Liturgy of St. Basil. Trans. by Holy Cross Seminary Press)

Run steady today!

January 3

A Spiritual Inventory

*Then went out to him Jerusalem and all Judea and all the region about the Jordan, and they were baptized by him in the river Jordan, **confessing their sins.***
—*Matthew 3:5–6 (Gospel from Royal Hours of Epiphany)*

*C*hrist is born! Glorify Him!

St. John the Forerunner was known as the *Baptist*, because he was baptizing people in the River Jordan. In the Jewish faith, one entered the faith through the ritual of circumcision. Periodically thereafter, people went to be ritually cleansed (washed) of their sins through baptism. This ritual was done throughout one's life—it was not a one-time thing. St. John had a large group of disciples; people who were going to him out in the desert at the River Jordan, to have him offer this ritual of baptism for them.

The initiation into the Christian faith is now done through baptism, not through circumcision. Baptism now is a one-time event that brings one into the Christian faith. Baptism is not repeated, there is no such thing as a re-baptism. What makes a baptism a baptism is that the name of the Holy Trinity—Father, Son, and Holy Spirit—is invoked over the person being baptized. Water is usually (not always—in an emergency baptism, one can invoke the name of the Trinity over someone without water and this is considered a valid baptism) involved and the person being baptized is usually immersed in the water three times. In some cases, water is poured over them instead.

We are baptized for three reasons: First, because we imitate the baptism of Christ by being baptized ourselves. Second, because He told us we must be born of "water and the spirit" in order to enter into the Kingdom of God (John 3:5). Third, because He commissioned the Church to "make disciples of all nations, baptizing them." (Matt. 28:19)

Baptism marks our entry into the Christian life. Baptism gives us the potential to receive salvation, but does not guarantee salvation. Baptism doesn't mean that we will live a life without sin. Baptism cleanses us from sin, and our baptismal state is the way we should strive to live, and especially end, our lives. In a fallen world, this is not possible. So we have a sacrament called confession and this sacrament allows us to return to the state we were in at baptism.

Baptism replaces the circumcision of the Old Testament. Confession replaces the baptism that John was doing. It is a periodic "washing" of our sins through "tears" of repentance. Confession takes us back to the state we were in at baptism, by cleansing the soul and restoring it to a state of purity. Confession allows us to own up for our sins, to be loosened from guilt, to reaffirm our faith in God, and to receive guidance and counseling through a spiritual father, so that our confession can be a true repentance, a plan to change our lives to point away from the sins we have confessed and towards God.

The sacrament of confession is found in John 20:23, where Christ tells His Disciples, "If you forgive the sins of any, they are forgiven; if you retain the sins of any, they are retained." This directive is passed on to the bishops and priests of today, the gift and the responsibility to lead the faithful to repentance and restoration through the sacrament of confession.

Confession ends with a prayer: "Have no further anxiety about the sins you have confessed but depart in peace." There are many times we pray to God, even confess to Him our sins, but we still feel anxious about them and we have no peace. Confession is given to us as a gift to take away guilt and anxiety, and restore the peace of God to each person.

The mechanics of confession involve making an appointment with a priest, making a list of the sins you wish to confess and receive guidance for, and then going with a humble and sincere heart, making your confession, getting some advice, and most importantly receiving absolution for your sins, a complete wiping out of them. As a priest who hears confessions, one my greatest joys is imparting absolution to those who come to confession. Just so you know, I remember virtually nothing of what I hear. I do not think less of people. To the contrary, confession generally brings priest and penitent closer together, not farther apart.

Everyone should go to confession at least once a year—it can be at any time. Like going to the doctor, you go when you are acutely sick, and you go once a year for a routine checkup. Confession should be handled in the same way—at times of acute spiritual sickness, and at least once a year for a routine spiritual checkup.

As we begin a new year, it is a good idea to take stock of where you are, to take stock of your sins and bad habits, and then consider whether this is a good time for you to go to confession, so that you can be rid of anxiety and depart in peace.

> By the greatness of Your mercy, You, O Savior, showed Yourself to sinners and publicans. Where else was Your light to shine, if not among those who sit in darkness. Glory to You. (Hymn from the Vespers of Epiphany. Trans. by Fr. Seraphim Dedes)

Have a Spiritually healthy day!

January 4

The Voice in the Wilderness

*As it is written in the book of the words of Isaiah the Prophet, "**The voice of one crying in the wilderness:** Prepare the way of the Lord, make His paths straight. Every valley shall be filled, and every mountain and hill shall be brought low, and the crooked shall be made straight, and the rough ways shall be made smooth; and all flesh shall see the salvation of God."*
—Luke 3: 4–6 (Gospel from Vesperal Liturgy of Epiphany)

*C*hrist is born! Glorify Him!

St. John the Baptist was the last of the Prophets. For hundreds of years prior to the Incarnation, the prophets encouraged God's people by foretelling that a Messiah was coming who would save the people from their sins and point them back to Paradise. St. John was the last of the Prophets because he announced that the time of the Messiah was at hand.

St. John, like the Virgin Mary and Jesus, was also born in a miraculous way. His parents, Zacharias and Elizabeth, were not able to have children. Yet, in old age Zacharias was told by the Archangel Gabriel that he and Elizabeth were going to have a son and that their son would be the Forerunner of Christ, the one who would prepare the way for the Christ to come immediately following.

St. John lived in the wilderness, where he was baptizing people. He was also preaching to the people to prepare the way of the Lord. St. John was "the voice of one crying in the wilderness." His voice was known. It was trusted and respected by his many followers. It was even respected by his enemies.

He was a voice of one. There were no others like him. His voice was solitary, but it was powerful. It didn't take many voices to preach of the coming of Christ. His powerful voice traveled far and inspired many. And he was "crying in the wilderness"—the wilderness is a lonely and desolate place. It is filled with danger.

Despite the fact that I live in a large city, I've always related to this passage. Because no matter where we live, we live in a wilderness of sin and uncertainty. All around there seems to be danger and spiritual desolation. If you don't believe me, just open a newspaper or turn on the TV news. A drive down the highway reveals dozens of pornographic billboards; eavesdropping on almost any conversation and you are bound to hear foul language. Even TV shows on the Family Channel are not very wholesome. And sometimes, it feels like the church, or Christians, or priests are "a voice of one crying in the wilderness," as it feels like sometimes the whole world is against the message of Christianity.

Here is where St. John serves as a role model to us. He wasn't well educated. He wasn't well dressed—he "wore a garment of camel's hair, and a leather girdle around his waist; and his food was locusts and wild honey (Matt. 3:4)." And he wasn't concerned how his message would be received. He understood that his role was to "cry" out the message. He wasn't going to coerce others into believing, only to make sure he was sending the message.

Many people were ready to receive Christ because of St. John. Many came to believe in Christ through his witness. St. John did not have a good end to his earthly life. He was beheaded—he became the first person to die for Christ. And yet he remains the most honored of the male saints of our church. He is featured prominently in every Orthodox Church, on the icon screen next to the icon of Christ. An icon of the Deisis shows Jesus Christ on a throne, with the Virgin Mary to His right and St. John to His left.

We are all called to be like St. John. Our voices are supposed to be heard in the wilderness. Our voices are supposed to talk about Christ. Like St. John, we are supposed to live in joyful expectation of Christ coming again in glory. Like St. John, we are supposed to be undeterred if our message is not heard, or even ridiculed. And like St. John, we are supposed to cry out even to our last breath, even if our life is short, even if our end is painful.

We are living in a world where the wilderness is trying to overwhelm the message, where society thinks if it can put up enough trees, the messenger will be silenced. We must be like St. John, we must boldly proclaim the message, we must boldly preach Christ, we must boldly and confidently witness for Christ.

Before we can cry out about Christ to others, however, we have to cry out for Christ to be in us. We have to cultivate Christ in us. We have to go to the "wilderness," to get away from the business of life, so that we can contemplate the things of Christ. Read the message in scripture, offer daily prayers, look for opportunities to help others daily, love one another, forgive one another, and you are well on your way to being a prophet like St. John. We are voices who must continue crying—the world needs Christ more than ever. If we are not going to talk about Him, who is?

> At the voice of one crying in the wilderness: prepare the
> way of the Lord! You have come, Lord, in the form of a
> servant. You are free from sin, yet You desire to be bap-
> tized by John! The waters saw You and were afraid; the

Forerunner cried out with trembling and said: "How shall the lamp illumine the Light? How shall the servant place his hand on the Master? Savior, as You take away the sin of the world, sanctify both me and the waters." (Hymn from the Blessing of the Waters. Trans. Fr. Seraphim Dedes)

Cry out to God today in prayer! Witness to God today in your actions.

January 5

Live Right!

For the grace of God has appeared for the salvation of all men, training us
to renounce irreligion and worldly passions and to live sober, upright and
*godly lives in this world, **awaiting our blessed hope**, the appearing of the*
glory of our great God and Savior Jesus Christ.
—*Titus 2:11–13 (Epistle from Liturgy of Epiphany)*

No one likes to be told to wait. We tend to want things, as one restaurant ad puts it, "your way, right away." Today's reflection is on the importance of waiting.

Lots of people can't wait to get married. Literally, they can't wait. So they start playing house in high school, experimenting with activities that are supposed to be reserved for marriage. They give of themselves not only in inappropriate sexual ways but also inappropriate emotional ways. When they've had their hearts broken too many times, when they've become so confused about things like love and intimacy, then when the time comes to have the reward in marriage, they are either not ready to have it or incapable of enjoying it properly. Many marriages are doomed from the start because neither party comes into marriage with a solid foundation.

Years ago, you had to amass 20 percent of the price of a house to put as a down payment in order to buy a house. You had to save, and usually that meant waiting, and being disciplined with your money. I remember as a newlywed we had very little money; we ate a lot of macaroni and cheese and frozen pizza those first couple of years. We didn't eat at fancy restaurants or buy expensive clothes. We didn't run up credit card debt. We saved as much as we could. We also never failed to offer stewardship to the church. After five years of marriage, we had saved enough and we bought our first house. As we walked into "our house" the day we closed on it, we were both in tears, because we knew what it had taken in order to get to that point—all the sacrifice and saving to get a place of our own to call our home.

When you hand something to someone, they don't value it as much. There was a period of time after we bought our home when banks decided that you could buy a house and put no money down on it, that everyone was entitled to a house, whether they had saved or not. So, many people bought houses who couldn't afford them. People bought houses putting no money down on them, so they were easy to walk away from when people got tired of making payments. People didn't have much stake in the houses and so they didn't invest much time or money in them. This led to a housing crisis that we're still trying to recover from, because we messed with the system that required people to wait and to save.

These two examples—dating and home buying—emphasize the importance of patiently waiting. They also emphasize that there is a reward for those who patiently wait. If you don't wait in order to experience marriage in the way God intended for you to experience marriage, then when it is time to get married, the experience will not be what it was supposed to be—you'll find that you haven't really learned how to be patient and loyal because you made a habit of not developing either in your relationships. And if you are not disciplined to save money, you won't delight in the joy of home ownership.

The message for today is simple—God is calling us to live upright and godly lives in this world, while awaiting our reward. It's hard to do this in a world where there is so much instant gratification, where we are told we don't have to wait for things.

God has shown us the path to salvation. We don't get there in one day. Life on earth is long for most people, and that's a good thing. That's lots of time to *save* for eternal life; that's lots of time to enjoy the things of the world also. When we were saving for a house, that didn't mean we had no fun—it just meant that we tempered our fun into outing that didn't cost that much. And when dating, that doesn't mean don't have any fun either—it means enjoying certain activities, while refraining from others.

The key to waiting is to first focus on the reward. And second, to have patience. The reward for a life well lived in the eyes of God is eternal life in the Kingdom of God. We lose focus on that because the world tells us it's not real. The world tells us not to worry about the future, to get all you can today! That's why you've got to pray and read scriptures and GET AROUND PEOPLE who believe as you do, so that you can have your confidence boosted that heaven is FOR REAL!!! And that it's worth *saving* in order to be *saved*.

And while waiting, we must do so with patience—we must patiently follow the commandments of God, which call us to sober, upright lives, not crazy, chaotic ones. God's commandments call us to save for the future, not put ourselves in spiritual debt or spiritual peril. Christ teaches us that the future reward is seeing the glory of God. God's glory—remember the Nativity—the shepherds saw it because they trusted. The Magi trusted and saw it too. Bethlehem was raucous and distracted. The parties and family reunions were probably a lot of fun. But they MISSED Christ, they missed God's glory, because they were focused on the "world."

Faith, trust, patience—these are the things that help us live sober, upright and Godly lives in this world. And the Godly life in this world, leads to glimpses of God's glory in this life and an everlasting experience of God's glory in the life to come. This is our *blessed hope*.

> The right hand of the Forerunner and Baptist, the prophet honored above all the prophets, trembled as he beheld You, for You are the Lamb of God Who cleanses the sins of the world! He was seized with fear and he cried: I dare not touch Your head, O Word! In Your mercy sanctify and enlighten me: For You are the Life and the Light and the peace of the world. (From the Royal Hours of Epiphany. Trans. by Fr. Seraphim Dedes)

Live in a Godly way today!

January 6

The Manifestation of God

*And when **Jesus** was baptized, He went up immediately from the water, and behold, the heavens were opened and He saw the **Spirit of God** descending like a dove, and alighting on Him; and lo, **a voice from heaven**, saying "**This is my beloved Son**, with whom I am well pleased."*
—Matthew 3:16–17 (Gospel of Epiphany)

The Feast we celebrate on January 6 is known by several names. One is the *Baptism of Christ*. This commemorates an event where Jesus Christ received baptism at the hands of St. John the Baptist, taking part in a ritual that was part of the Jewish faith. Even though He had no sin, and thus did not need this ritual washing, He was fulfilling the conditions of the Law, even as He prepared to supersede them in His ministry.

The most commonly used name for today's feast is *Epiphany*. If you look up the word epiphany in the dictionary, it means that something previously hidden or unknown is revealed. For example, through some intense life experience, a person might have an epiphany about what they are supposed to do with their life, or what life is all about. Sometimes this is called a light-bulb moment. Epiphany is the revelation of Jesus as the Christ, the Messiah, and is the first public act of Christ's ministry. Up until this point in history, the "Messiah" was written about in prophecy. This is the moment that the prophecy was fulfilled, the announcement of the Son of God to the whole world. (Of course, the prophecies were fulfilled with Christ's Incarnation but that event was not witnessed by many.)

The most powerful term used for today's feast is the *Theophany*, for this refers not only to the appearance of Christ, but the revelation of the rest of the Holy Trinity. To this point in these reflections, we have focused most specifically on Jesus Christ. At the moment of Christ's baptism in the Jordan by St. John the Baptist, the Spirit of God alighted on His head in the form of a dove, and a voice was heard from heaven, saying "This is my beloved Son, with whom I am well pleased." (Matt. 3:17) The voice of the Father gives endorsement to the Son, who is about to begin His earthly ministry. This establishes the relationship between God the Father and God the Son. It also establishes the presence of the Holy Trinity towards mankind, as for the first time in human history, all are made known to people at the same time. Just as it was at the Creation of the world, all three are present for the "re-creation" of the world, through the baptism of Christ, which not only manifests the Holy Trinity, but re-consecrates Creation. .

As we mark this feast of the manifestation of God at the baptism of Christ, let us spend a few moments speaking of God the Father and God the Holy Spirit. In previous reflections, we have examined the names given to God the Son—Word, Son of Man, Son of God, Messiah, Savior, Jesus Christ, etc. Let us make comment on the names of the Father and the Spirit as well.

Jesus reveals God as "Father": "For I have not spoken on My own authority; the **Father** who sent Me has Himself given Me commandment what to say and what to speak (John 12:49)."

God is revealed as Creator: "The Lord is the everlasting God, the **Creator** of the ends of the earth." (Is. 40:28)

God is called the "Almighty": "When Abraham was ninety-nine years old, the Lord appeared to Abram, and said to him, 'I am God **Almighty**; walk before Me, and be blameless.'" (Gen. 17:1)

Jesus called God the Father "Abba": "And He said, '**Abba,** Father, all things are possible to Thee; remove this cup from Me; yet not what I will, but what Thou wilt.'" (Mark 14:26)

God the Father is never seen: "No one has ever seen God; the Only Son, who is in the bosom of the Father, He has made Him known." (John 1:18) But the Father speaks and is heard. At the baptism: "And lo, a voice from heaven, saying, 'This is my beloved Son, with whom I am well pleased.'" (Matt. 3:17) And at the Transfiguration: "And a cloud overshadowed them, and a voice came out of the cloud, 'This is my beloved Son; listen to Him.'" (Mark 9:7)

The Holy Spirit is known as the Counselor (in some translations He is referred to as the Comforter, and the Paraclete): "But the **Counselor**, the Holy Spirit, whom the Father will send in My name, He will teach you all things, and bring to Your remembrance all that I have said to you (John 14:26)."

The Holy Spirit is also unseen but is made known in various ways. At the baptism, He appears as a dove: "And when Jesus came up out of the water, immediately He saw the heavens opened and the Spirit descending upon Him like a dove (Mark 1:10)." At Pentecost, He appears as fire:

And suddenly a sound came from heaven like the rush of
a mighty wind, and it filled all the house where they were
sitting. And there appeared to them tongues of fire, dis-
tributed and resting on each one of them. And they were
all filled with the Holy Spirit and began to speak in other
tongues, as the Spirit gave them utterance. (Acts 2:24)

We began these reflections with the Creation of the world, how all
three persons of the Trinity were present from before Creation and how
all co-created everything that was created. The first chapter of humanity
was the Old Testament, which included the Creation, the Fall, and the
Prophecies of a Savior. Faith was based on the "old covenant" with God,
based on commandments and laws.

The next chapter of humanity is the period of the New Testament,
which includes the ministry of Christ, the New Covenant, and the path
to salvation opened by the Crucifixion and Resurrection. The prologue
to this chapter is the Incarnation, which was, as we now know, a relatively
quiet affair. Jesus grew up as every other boy of His time did. The time of
preparation now over, Jesus is revealed as the Christ to all of humanity,
and thus begins His public ministry. The "re-creation" of the world is
begun with His baptism. There is even a tradition that holds that the
Jordan River reversed its course when Christ stepped into it, because the
waters were afraid and in awe. And the "re-creation" begins as the Creation
did, with an action of the Holy Trinity—Father, Son and Holy Spirit.

As You were baptized in the Jordan, O Lord, then the
worship of the Trinity became manifest, for the voice of
the Father bore witness to You, naming You the beloved
Son; and the Spirit, in the form of a dove, confirmed

the certainty of the word. O Christ God, who appeared and illumined the world, glory to You. (Apolytikion of Epiphan., Trans. by Fr. Seraphim Dedes)

Show the world how God has manifested Himself in your life!

January 7

It's all about HIM!!!

*The next day he saw Jesus coming toward him and said, "Behold the Lamb of God, who takes away the sin of the world! This is He of whom I said, "After me comes a man who ranks before me, for **He was before me."***
—John 1:29–30 (Gospel from Feast of St. John the Baptist)

oday is the feast of St. John the Baptist. (In Orthodox practice, when there is a major feast day, the day after the feast day is the day we commemorate the secondary figure of the feast. January 6 commemorates the Baptism of Christ, and January 7 commemorates St. John the Baptist. We know that St. John the Baptist was a cousin of Jesus, born to Elizabeth (and Zacharias) who was a cousin to the Virgin Mary. And that as he grew up, he began his work as the forerunner of Christ. He was baptizing people not only in the Jordan River but at "Aenon, near Salim (John 3:23);" presumably in other places as well. John had a group of disciples and also others who were curious as to who he was. In John 1, we read about how John told everyone that he was not the Christ, and endorsed Jesus as the Christ:

> And this is the testimony of John, when the Jews sent priests and Levites from Jerusalem to ask him, "Who are you?" He confessed, he did not deny, but confessed "I am

not the Christ." And they asked him "What then? Are you Elijah?" He said, "I am not." "Are you the prophet?" And he answered, "No." They said to him then, 'Who are you? Let us have an answer for those who sent us. What do you say about yourself?" He said, "I am the voice of one crying in the wilderness, 'Make straight the way of the Lord' as the prophet Isaiah said" . . ." I baptize with water; but among you stands One whom you do not know, even He who comes after me, the thong of Whose sandal I am unworthy to untie" . . ." I saw the Spirit descend as a dove from heaven, and it remained on Him. I myself did not know Him; but He who sent me to baptize with water said to me, 'He on whom you see the Spirit descend and remain, this is He who baptizes with the Holy Spirit.' And I have seen and have borne witness that this is the Son of God" . . . The next day again John was standing with two of his disciples; and he looked at Jesus as He walked, and said "Behold, the Lamb of God!" The two disciples heard him say this, and they followed Jesus. (John 1:19–37)

John knew that he was not the Christ. He knew that his role was to prepare the way for Christ, to steer others towards Christ. He knew that his role was to give glory to Christ. Along the way, John had disciples and his own amount of popularity, but he tempered that by constantly referring to Christ, "After me comes a man who ranks before me, for He was before me (John 1:29)."

In John 3:25–30 we read:

> Now a discussion arose between John's disciples and the Jews over purifying. And they came to John, and said to him, "Rabbi, He who was with you beyond the Jordan, to Whom you bore witness, here He is, baptizing, and all are going to Him." John answered, "No one can receive anything except what is given him from heaven. You yourselves bear me witness, that I said, I am not the Christ, but I have been sent before Him. He who has the bride is the Bridegroom; the friend of the Bridegroom, who stands and hears Him, rejoices greatly at the Bridegroom's voice; therefore this joy of mine is now full. **He must increase, but I must decrease."**

If we really believe that "every good and perfect gift (James 1:17)" comes from God, then we need to look very seriously at the role of John the Baptist, and adopt this role for our lives. I have a healthy ego, sometimes it is too big. But one thing that I TRY to do when someone gives me a compliment, is to try to say "Thank God" instead of saying "Thank you." I try to infer instead of "Thank YOU for complimenting ME" to infer "Thank You God who allowed me to do the thing for which I am being thanked."

As we wind up this series of reflections, again we go to the beginning, and that very first sin of ingratitude. If it's all about God and not about us, then we are thanking God for His blessings constantly. We are decreasing in our own sense of self-importance and letting Him increase in us. We are giving glory to God for our successes rather than attributing every good thing to ourselves.

In dying for our sins, Christ made it all about us. After all, who is going to die as an act of ego? Death is painful and it is permanent. In dying for us, Christ made it all about US and not about Him. In living for Christ, we have to make it all about Him and not about us. Our successes should be for His glory. Even our struggles should be done in a way that gives Him glory. We should look to Him even in our failures. John the Baptist was so correct in preparing the way of the Lord. The way we prepare the way for Him in our own hearts is to see Him as the bridegroom and see ourselves as the bride—to rejoice in Him, to submit to Him, to become one with Him.

In order for Him to increase in us, we (our egos, our ingratitude, our sinful tendencies) must decrease. That is a challenge for sure. As John says though, when He increases and we decrease, this is when our joy is the most filled. This takes faith and this takes discipline. As we are still in the early stages of a new year, reflect on specific ways that He can increase in you. Even by overtly saying "Thank God" often, you are giving glory to God and witness that He is working in you.

It's interesting when you watch sports, there are certain athletes who when they do something amazing point towards themselves, like "yeah, I'M all that." And there are others who point a finger to the heavens, ostensibly giving God the glory. When you make a mistake, learn to point the finger at yourself, asking forgiveness and pledging to do better. When you have a success, point the finger upward at God—it's all about Him. We are here because of Him. We have the potential to be saved because of Him. We have talents because He gave them to us. Our purpose in life is to honor Him. Our entrance into heaven is up to Him. And if we are blessed to go to heaven, it will be all about being one with Him. Find a way to honor Him each and every day!

Saint of God, intercede for us. Coming from the desert, the Forerunner's voice to all points out the Word who for our sake has visited us bodily; full of joy he prepares himself to baptize Him who has arrived, the one who purifies our souls from the ancestral sin through faith in Him. (9th ode of the Orthros of the Feast of St. John the Baptist. Trans. by Fr. Seraphim Dedes)

Make it all about Him today!

Epilogue

We Have Seen the Light

*The land of Zebulun and the land of Naphtali, towards the sea, across the Jordan, Galilee of the Gentiles—**the people** who sat in darkness **have seen a great light**, and for those who sat in the region and shadow of death, Light has dawned." From that time Jesus began to preach saying "Repent, for the kingdom of heaven is at hand."*
—Matthew 4:16–17 (Gospel from Sunday after Epiphany)

Wow, what a journey we have had. We've prepared for and celebrated two great feasts of the Nativity and Theophany. We have brought our gifts to the manger and have seen the Lord as a baby. We have stood on the banks of the Jordan River and have seen the Trinity revealed.

Having gone through this journey, I pray that you have seen more of Christ's Light, that there is less "darkness" and mystery about the Incarnation, and that there is now more "light" and therefore joy, as you hopefully now understand more.

I have studied the Nativity as I never have before. I know more than I ever did before about this great feast. I thank God for His inspiration in writing this series. I thank Him for those who have encouraged and helped me along the way. I thank Him for those who are reading this message, and I thank YOU who are reading this message. I thank you for your prayers and for your encouragement.

Our journey to salvation does not end today. Our pursuit of knowledge of God does not end. Neither does our desire to grow in faith.

The last verse of the Gospel we cover for today gives us a goal for every day of our lives. "Repent!" Repentance is a continual, not a one-time change in our orientation so that we are growing ever closer to Christ. Repentance is a continual refocusing of our efforts to grow towards Him and away from sinful tendencies.

Why do we need to continue to repent? Because repentance is the way we grow closer to Christ. And why is *that* important? Because "The Kingdom of heaven is at hand."

In the span of eternity, our life on this earth is a small blip in time. Our judgment to be found worthy of God's Kingdom is just around the corner. Even if you are destined to live for many more years (and NO ONE knows that for sure), in the span of eternity, the end of your earthly life is just around the bend. This is a big motivation to repent, to change and grow; knowing that at the end of life there is a judgment that is between us and the kingdom of God. Many will fall short and be judged worthy of condemnation rather than salvation.

"The Kingdom of Heaven is at hand" is not just an end-of-our-life thought. The Kingdom of Heaven is at hand means that we can experience the Kingdom TODAY!!! It is as close as a prayer. You can open the Bible and be in the Kingdom. You can love another person and be there. You can go to church and worship. You can touch the Divine God through Holy Communion. Through Christ's love, you can be in the Kingdom from NOW and to eternity.

However, just because you have Christ, just because you repent, and even though you may experience God's kingdom frequently that does not mean there won't be difficult days or dark times. With Christ though, those dark times never defeat the Light that is Christ. In John 1:5, we read that His "Light shines in the darkness and the darkness has not overcome it." In John 11:9–10, Jesus tells us, "If any one walks in the day, he does not stumble, because he sees the light of this world. But if any one walks in the night he stumbles, because the light is not in him."

We are not in darkness. We have seen the Light. Let us do the work of the Lord today. Let us continue to pray for one another, support one another, and love one another. So that one day we can all be in His Heavenly Kingdom!

> Our Savior, grace and truth, appeared in His Epiphany
> in the streams of the Jordan; and those who lay once in
> the dark and shadow He illumined now. He has come
> and appeared, the Light unapproachable. (Kontakion of
> Epiphany. Trans. by Fr. Seraphim Dedes)

To Him be the glory to the ages of ages. Amen.

CPSIA information can be obtained
at www.ICGtesting.com
Printed in the USA
BVHW041655071122
651358BV00005B/89